PACKRAT PAPERS
VOLUME 1
(Revised Edition)
$3.95

EDITED BY BETTY MUELLER
BOOK DESIGN & ARTWORK BY TOM MCMACKIN

OTHER PUBLICATIONS BY SIGNPOST:

BOOKS

BACKPACKING WITH BABIES AND SMALL CHILDREN,
  by Goldie Silverman

BOULDERS AND CLIFFS, by Dallas Kloke

KAYAK AND CANOE TRIPS IN WASHINGTON,
  by Werner Furrer

NORTHWEST FORAGING, by Doug Benoliel

PACIFIC CREST TRAIL HIKE PLANNING GUIDE,
  by Chuck Long

PACIFIC CREST TRAIL IN WASHINGTON (HIGH TRAILS),
  by Louise Marshall

ROCK CLIMBING GUIDE, LEAVENWORTH AND INDEX,
  by Rich Carlstad and Don Brooks

SNOW TOURS IN WESTERN WASHINGTON,
  by Randy J. McDougall

WATER TRAILS OF WASHINGTON, by Werner Furrer

WINTER WALKS AND SUMMER STROLLS,
  SEATTLE AND EVERETT,
  by Louise Marshall

WINTER WALKS AND SUMMER STROLLS,
  SKAGIT, WHATCOM, SAN JUAN, AND ISLAND COUNTIES,
  by Fred Darvill, M.D., and Louise Marshall

MAGAZINE

SIGNPOST NEWS-MAGAZINE for Northwest backpackers and
other trail travelers. Write for a sample copy.

Signpost Publications
16812 - P 36th Ave. W
Lynnwood, WA   98036

Signpost Publications welcomes inquiries from authors about
prospective books.

ISBN 0-913140-14-7

PACKRAT PAPERS

VOLUME 1
(REVISED EDITION)

TIPS ON EQUIPMENT (and other stuff) FOR CAMPERS, BACKPACKERS, AND THOSE WHO TRAVEL LIGHTLY

ACKNOWLEDGEMENTS

How can one acknowledge all who have helped to build a packrat's nest? This collection of packrat papers is the sum of the efforts of many who, over the first 10 years of The Signpost's existence, have shared their know-how with others.

Only those whose contributions took the form of full-length articles or multi-paragraph pieces are credited by name in these pages. A far greater number of persons sent in smaller items.

Signpost Publications joins its readers in offering thanks to all for the willingness of each contributor to share his or her knowledge.

CONTENTS

Packrat Papers, Volume 2, is the companion to this book. In it our packrat shares its cache of "treasures" on subjects like **Eating Know-How, In-Camp Paraphernalia, Safety & Survival,** and **Wilderness Care.**

INTRODUCTION

It is generally understood that the little packrat is an animal which gathers all sorts of materials -- whatever catches its fancy. It hoards these objects in its nesting place in a great pile of mixed debris.

When you open a packrat's nest, you expect to find that some of the collection is worthless, and some is useful. This is a matter of personal opinion, for the packrat which gathered it treasured it all.

The collection of information in these pages forms a veritable packrat's nest of lore for the hiker, camper, and snow tourer. It has been gathered by a sort of team of hikers/packrats, who contributed it, item by item, to be published in the pages of The Signpost. Items which appeared to be of lasting interest were selected for reprinting in this collection.

*　　*　　*

The Signpost is a newsmagazine for hikers and other self-powered trail users in the Pacific Northwest. Founded in 1966, it is the oldest general circulation periodical in the hiking field.

NEW BOOTS - The foundation on which all hiking, backpacking and climbing enjoyment is built is definitely a good-fitting pair of boots. Nothing else can give as much pleasure or pain, and yet all too few people really know how to select the proper pair of boots for their needs. It is almost impossible to tell another individual what pair of boots to buy, but guidelines can be given to assist in making the choice.

The first determination to be made is where and for what purposes the boots will be used. Just as the occasional day hiker and the expedition climber have different requirements, so do the backpacker of 6-8 summer weekends and the year-round practitioner. The trail traveler does not require as much from a boot as the cross-country packer or climber. The amount of protection and expected usage will tell you what you need. Most people tend to go to one extreme or the other. For the novice the variety of boots is certainly bewildering, but at least it gives one a choice and a chance to find a fit for both foot and budget.

The sole of your boot should be a lug-type that will provide the traction necessary on any kind of trail or cross-country terrain. It should be firm enough to wear well. The most popular soles are Vibram, which come in two weights: Roccia, the light, soft, flexible sole with shallow tread; and Montagna, a firmer, deeper tread. The firmer tread will give more protection.

There are also other soles available. Many less expensive boots, of which waffle stompers are one type, have soft rubber soles with tread designs to simulate Vibram soles but without the wear qualities. For extra long life in soles and the protection that goes along with it, the Malo 2 sole is firmer and longer lasting than Vibram.

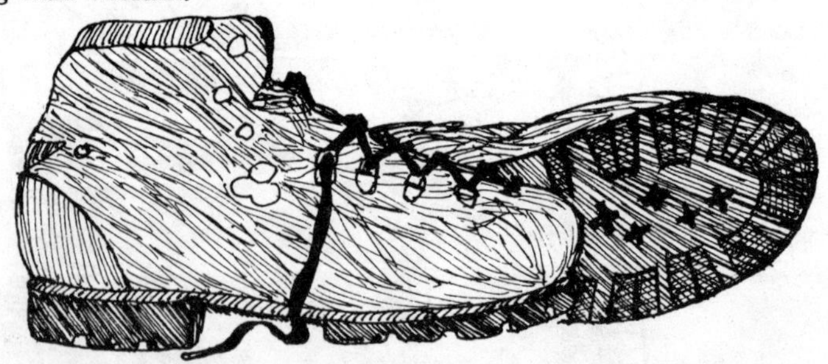

Above the sole should be a layer of leather. This midsole will vary in thickness, depending on how much protection is desired for the sole of your foot. The rougher the ground you will be walking on, the greater the weight you carry, the more protection you will need. A steel shank is often added at this point to strengthen the sole and support the arch. This portion of the boot is very important for preventing bruises to the soles of the feet, a most painful affliction when suffered many miles from the road. Ideally, enough midsole is wanted to protect your feet on the type of terrain you plan to hike, but no more than necessary because extra weight can be a real burden.

The leather tops of your boots are another important part of the system for protecting your feet. The more you and your equipment weigh, the more work they will have to do. Whether the leather has a smooth side out or a rough side out is not of great importance. Some excellent boots today have plastic outside that is even more durable than leather. The important consideration here is that if you have a rough out leather top it should not be split too thin, or you will not get the protection, support and life you need. The uppers should be attached to the soles by stitched welt construction, and many of the more expensive boots are double or triple stitched.

When fewer seams are used in the construction of uppers, there are fewer places for water to get into your boots. This is usually reflected in the price tag of the boot also. The height of your boots can vary from about 6" to 8", depending on the protection you need. Boots come with or without elastic tops at the back of the ankle. The elastic is designed to keep out snow and loose rock. It works with varying success for different people. A pleated, sewed tongue will assist in keeping water and dirt out of the front of the boot.

Boots available in the stores today offer the choice of many different linings. If the lining is too thick it will be hot in the summer, but in winter it is good insulation against the cold. The addition of some padding around the top can make it much more comfortable on the ankle if you are not used to the higher type of footwear. The laces that usually come in a new pair of boots are not the best quality and need replacing with good nylon laces.

When you are ready to buy a pair of boots, where should you go? No single store can have the answer for everybody, so visit several stores and try on a variety of boots. Prices will vary from boot to boot and store to store, but generally plan to spend at least $30. An average boot runs from $50-$60, and beyond that the range goes up and up and up.

When trying on a boot, before lacing it up slide your foot as far forward as possible, and slip your forefinger down between your heel and the heel of the boot. If the boot is the proper size, it will be a snug fit with your finger. Next, lace the boot tightly and walk about the store for a few minutes. Then try kicking the toe against a kicking post (most stores have one) to see if your toes will touch the front of the boot. Another way to do this is to stand on the slope of the shoe fitting stool, but this is not as satisfactory as the kicking. If your toes touch the front of the boot when you hike, you will probably end up with some black and blue toenails. It is important to get the right fit. If your toes do touch when you kick the post, you could have too wide a boot so try a narrower one.

My experience (which is mostly limited to fitting boots to six family members) has led to the conclusion that about 20% of the time one cannot get a really good fit no matter how many boots are tried. Almost always, however, a fair fit can be obtained in one type of boot in some store. If this is your case, take the best one you can find and go with a happy mind because all is not lost. A pair of insoles can help you get a better fit.

So you have a new pair of boots, and now you can go hiking.
Well, almost. Boot manufacturers are making boots to sell. And
boots which have not been waterproofed look better, so they are
not waterproofed. I have found that a large can of Sno-Seal is
just about the right amount for a large pair of boots. You can get
about four applications from a can. Another type such as the
Leath-R-Seal should be used around the seams.

Now take a heat lamp or hair dryer in one hand and a boot
in the other, and apply heat only until the wax melts and you
see it soak into the leather. This method will prevent using too
much heat on the leather -- one of its worst enemies. Then
wear your new boots around the house and yard for a week or so
to condition them gradually. Next take a couple of easy, short
hikes that will break in the boots and not your feet.

If, at this point, you feel you do not have a completely
satisfactory fit, it is time to take the boots to a good boot repair
shop. Pour out your troubles to a responsible boot man; he will
glue a pad here and a strip of foam there. Lo and behold! The
boots become a friend of the foot! Although he cannot be expected to work miracles (it only seems that way), in my experience several pairs of boots have been saved -- and with them the
feet -- for many more glorious miles of backpacking.

From then on, it is a matter of proper care of your boots.
Vibram soles are designed for curvatures of the earth as well as
the feet. The soles will enhance that relationship if not abused
on city streets and cement. When backpacking try to have some
street shoes in your car, available right off the trailhead. You'll
save years on your Vibrams.

If necessary, Vibram soles can be replaced by certain shoe
repair shops for from $18-$21. An old hiking boot can be rejuve-
nated 100%. Or a pair of army combat boots from Goodwill
which fit well around the feet can be converted into fine hiking
boots by adding new Vibram soles.

Clean and dry boots after each trip. Dry them slowly, on a
boot tree if possible, at room temperature. Never use heat that
will destroy the life of the leather or shut them in a closet where
they can mildew. Apply Sno-Seal after each use until the origi-
nal can is empty and then as needed to maintain their waterproofness. With proper care, your boots should give you many
miles of carefree, blister-free hiking.

> -- Excerpts from an article, "Boots -- Friend or Foe,"
> by Brad Bradley

FLAT TONGUE - The tongue in my boots never seemed to lie down properly when the boots were laced. I was afraid snow might get in, so I had the shoemaker put in a lacing hook at the top of the tongue (the same kind of hook as those already on the boots, not one which leaves a hole through the leather.) My laces hook this when I lace the boots, and the tongue stays down.

MADE-TO-ORDER BOOTS - It is possible to find a company that makes loggers' boots and have them make something for you, but this has seldom proved successful. The resulting boots tend to be heavy, much heavier than is needed for hiking or climbing. There are such manufacturers all around in states where logging is big. This possibility may be worth a try.

Peter Limmer at Intervale, New Hampshire, is the only known outfit in the nation which actually is in the business of making hiking and climbing boots by hand and to order. They send you a description of what measurements they need, the purchaser does the measuring, and the Limmer family creates the desired foot gear. We understand that 95% of the time the result is satisfactory. If the boots do not fit well, they can be returned. One slight difficulty: There is about a year's wait to have Limmer boots made, and if the first effort is not a success the eager purchaser goes back to the bottom of the list for another year's wait.

One last possibility is to combine boot-hunting with a trip to Europe. Dave Page, a cobbler in Seattle, says that he maintains a list of six or eight people in Europe who do this work (it varies from year to year). For more information, contact him at 2101 North 34th Street, Seattle, WA 98103 (206/632-8686).

WHY BUY BANANA PEELS? - That's about what you'd be doing if you invested in PVC "traction-lugged" soles. PVC vinyl is slippery beyond belief on ice or packed snow. We're skeptical if even "traction-lugged" construction would provide traction . . . the banana-peel slipperiness wouldn't give those lugs time to take hold. We advise being very wary of ANY vinyl-soled footwear, regardless of any fine features they may have.

GI SWAMP BOOTS - Surplus stores carry used GI swamp boots at around $15 a pair. They have a medium lug sole bonded to a leather mid-section covering foot and heel. The ankle casing is heavy legging material sewed onto the leather. Advantages: Comfortable, lightweight, cool, fast-drying, warmer in winter when shoes get soaked by snow, and inexpensive. Disadvantages: Not lovely to look at, don't support ankles like all-leather tops.

BREAK-IN HELP - When breaking in boots, use ordinary rubbing alcohol on the inside and outside and let it evaporate. It softens the boots.

BREAKING-IN - A suggestion for breaking in boots -- leave the
top laces undone.   This helps prevent heel movement (and blisters) while the sole is still stiff.

PLASTIC CLIMBING BOOTS - A pair of plastic mountaineering
boots, lent to a British Columbia Mountaineering Club member,
proved to be unsuitable for mountaineering.   The results of the
trial (over 100 miles in varying terrain and weather conditions)
were reported in an issue of the club newsletter.   The skilled
climber who tried them said:
        "The crunch came on the Monarch Icecap where they were
worn for seven days of snow and ice climbing and never dried out
once.   When placed beside leather boots in the evening wind
(the only chance to dry boots there) the leather boots dried partially, the plastic boots not at all.   Stuffing them with wool or
newspaper somewhat eliminated surface moisture but the boots
were still wet and slimy in the morning.
        "Needless to say, on one occasion they raised a crop of
blisters and if it had been winter they probably would have cre-
ated more serious problems -- frostbite among them.   Drawbacks:
1) The boots do not breathe.   2) The soft leather tongue lets water through like a sieve although the rest of the boot is watertight.   3) The boots appear to enlarge rather than slowly form
themselves to the shape of the foot.   (This action was compared
with a newly purchased pair of leather boots which gradually
molded to the shape of the foot.) Good features: 1) The boots fit
well at first and needed no breaking in.   2) For day or short weekend hikes in summer they might be suitable after having a few
days to dry out. "

CORRECT WATERPROOFING - Boots should be thoroughly treated
with a good water repellent, both to keep them more comfortable
and to prolong their life.   Boots are made of two different kinds
of leather, vegetable tanned leather and dry tanned, or chrome
tanned, leather.
        The kind of treatment you use on your boots depends upon
the kind of leather.   Ask your shoe salesman if you don't know for
sure about your boots.   Most hiking boots are made from dry
tanned leather, since it is warmer, but several major lines (Red
Wing, for one) are made with vegetable tanned leather.
        Generally, plain wax such as Kiwi Polish can be used on
both kinds.   Vegetable tanned leathers should be treated with oils
or greases, like Huberd's Leather Dressing or Red Wing Shoe Oil.
Dry tanned leathers should be treated with waxes or silicone treatments.   Sno-Seal is a mixture of wax and silicone and is very appropriate for dry tanned leather (but apparently not for vegetable
tanned leather).   Never use oils or greases on dry tanned leathers.
They will clog the pores and destroy most of the leather's insulative qualities.
        Whatever kind of treatment you use, you must be careful to
keep oils or silicone treatments away from cemented seams, par-

ticularly around the sole of the boot. The oils and solvents in
the silicone solutions weaken the cement. Instead, use Leath-R-
Seal, which is a mixture of shellac and wax, or use plain wax in
those areas.

Epoxy sealants, available at most hardware stores, very effectively protect the welt and other seams from moisture and
abrasion. The sealants come in two parts. You mix them, then
dab the mixture on the areas you want to protect. Be careful
about getting the mixture on your skin, though; it is very caustic
and will raise some painful blisters.

Good boot care, then, is a little more complicated than
just smearing a bunch of goop on whenever you get around to it.
To get the maximum benefit from the effort you put into properly waxing, greasing or sealing your boots, do the job after you
get back from the hike rather than as a last minute rush job
squeezed in while waiting for your ride to show up.

-- Excerpts from an article, "Wet Hiking,"
by Rick Ells

WATCH IT WITH THE WATERPROOFING - A hiker had a pair of
boots in which the soles separated from the uppers. When she was
told it was the result of the way she waterproofed the boots, she
notified Signpost. The volunteer then turned in this report.

"Climbing boots, as opposed to hiking boots, are constructed with several layers in the upper sole to stiffen the sole. One
of these layers is leather. In a hiking boot the upper sole is all
rubber . . . If wax waterproofing such as Sno-Seal is applied
and the boot heated enough for the waterproofing to become liquid in form, the liquid will go into the leather layer of the sole
and soften it. The soft layer will then start to rub back and forth
against the other stiff layers in the sole. It is this rubbing back
and forth that tears the stitching.

"The leather part of the upper sole is the most valuable
part of the boot and needs special care. Recreational Equipment Co-op recommends using Leath-R-Seal on the welt portion of the boot and Sno-Seal on the upper portion. At no time
should the boot be put into an oven or exposed to extreme heat
(such as roasting at a campfire). Admittedly, opinions differ as
to the proper care of boots and as to the proper way of applying
waterproofing. REI feels the method described here is the most
effective."

SILICONE DRESSING - A silicone shoe-saver dressing designed
to make ordinary shoes waterproof has been found to work well
on hiking boots, too. One application is enough on new foot
gear. If applied on used shoes, clean them well first to remove
dirt or old polish.

EXTRA WATERPROOFING - A small discarded wide-mouth plastic prescription bottle, about 1x2", can be filled with wax waterproofing for boots. Cap securely, place in a small plastic bag, wrap a paper towel around it and place all in another small plastic bag. Tuck it into the pack along with the raingear. Then, on an occasion when the hiker awakens under tarp or tent to the drum of raindrops and all his world is very wet, he puts on his leg wear plus his chaps or rainpants. With his fingers he applies the wax waterproofing material liberally to his boots, then puts them on. He wipes his hands on the paper towel and contributes it to assist the morning fire. Feet will stay dry (longer). Caution: Sitting cross-legged on freshly waxed boots can be messy!

BOOT REPAIR - For temporary repair of delaminated boot sole, put heavy rubber band from inner tube over toe and tie behind heel with cord. Tape, cord or something else could be used for the toe band, but tension toward the heel is essential.

EMERGENCY BOOT REPAIR - On the Crest Trail in August we met one hiker whose boots were held together with rubberbands. He was on a long trip (British Columbia to Oregon) and his old boots just started falling apart. Something to think about before starting a longer trip. (Ed. comment: This report shows that it isn't only beginners who need to be reminded of the need for good footwear. On an 8-day backpack one summer, we watched a hiker's boots part company between soles and uppers, and that hiker was planning to continue immediately on a second 8-day trip. Luckily, in a large party, someone had a supply of wire, someone else had an awl, someone else knew something about shoe repair, and emergency repairs were effected. So we agree with the letter writer -- think about footwear before starting a longer backpack, and at least carry lots of strong rubberbands.)

CARRY SUPPLIES - On long trips in large groups, someone should carry shoe repair materials. Boot heels have been known to be pulled off by mud, and soles have come loose from uppers.

INSOLES - The Spenco footpad, made of two layers of material with a ball bearing-like relationship, gives comfort to the hiker. The top layer of the pad rolls around on the bottom layer, thus relieving the foot of this heat-producing friction.

MORE ON FEET - Tight, ankle-fitting boots will slide on much easier if you put a piece of waxed paper behind your heel when the boot is half on. A small patch of waxed paper around the heel, but under the outer sock, will also help prevent blisters.

BOOT LINERS - For boot liners, use the plastic trays your meat comes in from the grocery store. Makes them warmer, because of the insulating quality of the plastic.

UNFREEZING BOOTS - To warm up frozen boots, put them on with only one thin pair of socks. They will soon thaw out enough to accept the regular two pairs of heavy socks. Suggestion gleaned from "Give Me The Hills" by Miriam Underhill.

WARMING BOOTS - A few times I have tried putting hand warmers in my boots but found the warmers too unreliable. One usually goes out during the night. An issue of Field and Stream had an article on snow camping which suggested tieing boots together, draping them around your neck under your parka in the morning (wear booties). When breakfast is over, your boots will be ready to put on.

It takes several days to dry boots in the house. On a hike, I say just dump the water out and wear them.

DRYING BOOTS - To dry boots away from home, heat sand or gravel in skillet, pour into boots. Gravel is probably easier to remove later. This procedure is said to dry boots in 30 minutes.

BOOT TREES - Anyone having unexplainable foot blisters or toenail trouble would be wise to hold his boots at eye level and take a good look at the sole profile. A pronounced "rocking chair" look to the soles might be the problem. The curve comes as the result of putting boots away carelessly after a wet hike. The leather shrinks slightly in drying and pulls the soles up at the toe. The effect is especially noticeable in large sizes. The solution is to get an inexpensive boot tree with wing-nut, screw-down adjustments. After each hike, clamp the boots into the proper shape, then let them dry.

BODY RAIMENT

WOOL - For people who exert themselves outdoors there is nothing that equals wool! Wool does not lose its insulative properties if it becomes wet. A mountaineering friend, who has climbed some of the tallest, claims he wears only wool when trailing and saves his down for camp. Another friend, who worked on the early DEW line, reports that after trying various other materials, the government issued only wool clothing for anyone working in cold weather.

Wool has other virtues besides staying warm when wet. It is usually woven as a thick insulating cloth for outdoor use, thus it is more snagproof than the latest synthetics. The synthetics

are stronger as thread, but they are usually woven thinner and
my own experience has shown that they tear easier. While this
might not be important to downhill skiers, hikers and climbers
need more substantial clothing.

The U.S. Navy developed the multi-layer theory for keeping warm. Essentially this means that for the same weight, the
more layers of clothing the warmer you will be. Let me give
you an example. In the winter, in addition to going snowshoeing I go steelhead fishing. On the really cold winter mornings I
dress as follows:

First I put on wool undershirt and drawers (long johns).
These are no ordinary woolies, but something really special.
Mine are yellow colored Viking brand merino wool, which I've
only been able to get in Woodward's Department Store in Vancouver, British Columbia. They are made in England, are soft
as a cloud and scratch-free.

Then I put on a thin blue wool sleeveless sweater and three
(yes, three) thin wool shirts. Of course, my pants are wool, army surplus. Over the shirts I wear a thin nylon vinyl-coated
rain jacket to cut the wind.

A hat is very necessary as the Navy found that if your head
is covered it is easier for you to keep warm. In fact, I even
wear my Scotch wool cloth tam to bed; but that's another story.

Two pairs of socks, knee-high wool and nylon anklets, and
waders complete my fishing outfit. For overnight snowshoe
camping, the only change is to wear 9-hole laced rubber paks
with wool felt inner soles.
-- Excerpts from an article, "Up With Ruminant
Quadrupeds!" by David Schonbrun

FABRIC WARMTH - As to which type of cloth is warmest, some
people say there is no significant difference between the fibers
themselves in this respect. The difference lies in the way the
fibers can be made into fabrics. Wool cloth is recognized as
having the greatest capacity to fill its cells with air and, after
being emptied by pressure, to fill again repeatedly through a
long life. Acrylic fibers, especially the modacrylics, have
qualities similar to wool in many respects. Although they cannot
meet the resilience test to the same degree, they rate better on a
scale that favors saving money.

KEEPING WARM - The curious reaction of skin to cold that we
call "gooseflesh" is a hangover, some say, from the older days
of mankind when everyone had protective hair over most of the
body. Each hair root is set in muscles which automatically raise
and lower the hair according to atmospheric conditions. When
humans had more hair than clothes and the flesh became cold,
the hair would literally stand on end, providing a layer of still
air against the skin. And it is that layer of still air which is,
even today, the warmest thing we can wear.

For warmth we need a fabric or combination of materials that can trap and hold a layer of air near our bodies. Any fabric which is fuzzy, napped or woven with many tiny air cells will do it. Or a filling of feathers, down, bits of fiber or shredded foam, encased in fabric, will make that trap for air.

If the surrounding air is quiet, this kind of fabric or construction operates very well to hold an insulating layer against the body. If, however, the air is moving -- caused by the wind blowing -- a second defense is needed. This could be some kind of fabric, tightly woven but not airproof entirely, which would stop the cold moving air from penetrating the insulating layer.

WINDBREAKERS - The outer windbreaker jacket needed to prevent cold air from blowing away the insulating layer of still air next to the body can be suitably made of any of several fibers -- nylon, cotton, wool, or a combination of these and others. But laundering or dry cleaning information should be on the label.

WINTER ALTITUDES - For any hike above 4000 feet and in the winter months always, at least one complete layer of wool should be included in the gear -- hat, mittens, sweater, pants and socks. Also needed are a waterproof parka and pants (or chaps). These items are especially vital in locations where heavy rain or wet snowfall can be expected. Synthetics and down are pretty useless when wet.

CONSERVE WARMTH - Winters are long in the high country and conserving body heat is important. Some 40% of your body heat is lost from the head and neck, experts figure. Prevent this heat loss by wearing a turtle neck shirt, a scarf and a wool hat.

LAYER SYSTEM - Many people favor concentrating on several thin, warmish layers rather than a single heavy garment that is undeniably warm. For example: A person starts off in the morning wearing a cotton knit shirt, a lightweight sweater, a sweat- shirt and a nylon shell parka. As the day warms up, he peels off a layer at a time. If he wore just a shirt and a heavy jacket, he would be too cool if he took off the jacket and too warm if he left it on.

SNOW OVERPANTS - A pair of the Army surplus cotton-nylon blend pants work nicely as overpants on snowshoe trips. Replace the drawstrings at the ankles with elastic, because drawstrings are hard to untie when wet or icy. Many of us in the Vancouver, B. C. area are using the small Swedish snowshoes on steep terrain. These snowshoes, which don't drop away from your heel when you lift your foot, kick up a lot of snow and the overpants keep one's legs and seat dryer.

BAGGY PANT/KNICKERS

GETTING IT ALL TOGETHER - Clothing is important on the trail, but not in the way fashion dictates. The function of clothing is to protect the body from nature's wide range of inclement weather. Warmth and comfort are most important and no one gives a hoot about style.

Wool is basic to a good hiking wardrobe. Search through secondhand shops for a pair of all-wool hiking pants. If you cannot find the right size, try shrinking a pair to fit. Goodwill and Salvation Army stores often sell recycled Army pants and wool shirts for a pittance. But do start with woolen pants.

Next you can add woolen sweaters, hats and mittens. Then important things like string net underwear, a unique cocky hat, colorful shirts, and maybe skimpy hiking shorts or whatever, as you learn more about the demands of hiking in your area.

A windproof jacket and a good rain parka and pants soon assume considerable importance in the hiker's outfit. It is possible, but not quite as comfortable, to start with cheaper gear and learn as you go what fits your needs. Raingear also is available in kit form for home sewing (see Sew It Yourself). It takes from 5-10 hours of sewing time per parka, but the instructions and material are top quality. Sewing these kits at home saves roughly 40% of the cost of buying one.

If you want to be prepared for rock scrambling, hike in knickers. Shop around for baggy-legged woolen pants, often sold at sales, or get Air Force flying pants. A neat pair of knickers can easily be made at home. First, with the pants on bend your leg, and then mark the pants about 2-3" below the knee. Cut off the legs at that point, and open the outside seams 4-5" up. Make cuffs out of the leftover material, and sew them to the pantlegs so cuff front overlaps the back about 4". Velcro can be sewed to the overlapping parts for easy closure. Finished, you have a $30 pair of knickers.

If you wish to keep on making your own outfit, the logical next step is to knit a colorful pair of knicker socks. Many patterns are available. Some hikers prefer a knee sock without a heel or toe, but with an elastic over the instep. This way the sock need not get in the way of the sock combination that has been worked out to go with a particular pair of boots.

Another good type is the tube sock which can be knit without a heel. During World War II thousands of those were hand knit for the troops. You may be able to find someone who has an old knitting book with the pattern in it. With no fixed heel the sock can be turned a different way each time it is worn and no one spot receives most of the wear.

-- Excerpts from an article, "Getting Started,"
by Emilie Martin

KIDS' MITTEN LINERS - To make a mitten liner for little hands from an adult-sized liner, trace outline of the child's hand on larger liner, sew around the outline (leaving a little room for movement), then cut off the excess. This is useful if you can't get a liner to fit the child.

SOCKS RECYCLED - Mittens can be made from an expensive pair of wool socks with holes in the heels, to extend their usefulness. Cut out the heel and fashion a thumb out of excess material from the top of the sock or from another sock. Try to avoid seams where they would be bothersome.

WET NET A PROBLEM - I have found that cotton net undershirts sop up sweat so much that they can't be kept on when one stops for the day. And, short of drying by a fire, there seems to be no way to dry them. Would wool net shirts be better? Similar shirts made of a synthetic might not soak up as much and would be easier to dry, but don't seem to be available. In Europe ski racers wax their net shirts, and I would like to try this but don't know how to do it. (Ed. note: Wool net shirts, $9.95, REI Co-op, Seattle; polyester-cotton, top $4.65, bottom $4.95.)

WET NET SOLUTION - Jack Stephenson of Stephenson Warmlite writes: You only get wet from sweat if you're overheated. Thus the solution is very simple. At the first sign of dampness (usually underarms) open up your jacket, shirt or whatever is necessary to regulate temperature. You'll feel better, retain moisture and stay dry. Changing materials can't help, since that can only shift where the water might end up.

INSULATION - A set of ordinary quilted, insulated underwear is light, terrifically warm, easy to wear (no itch, no creep), and good for winter work outdoors. For hikers, such underwear protects against exposure in sudden storms and also can be used to prevent chill and shock in cases of injury. The top part of the underwear set can be worn as a light jacket.

NYLON UNDERWEAR - An advantage of nylon underwear is that it dries fast. Some doesn't, if it has cotton in it.

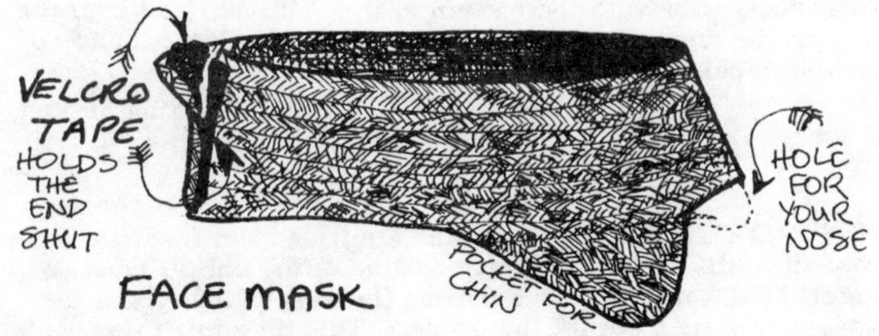

CROCHET A FACE MASK - These directions were developed by Elaine Smith, Seattle, to help a friend on a ski patrol who once suffered from frostbite. She has used acrylic yarn on occasion, but recommends wool for the most warmth. And, she adds, no one has complained of its being scratchy.

GAUGE - Approx. 4 st per inch, 4 rows per inch. Single crochet throughout. Size I or J hook, 4-ply wool yarn (3 masks per 4-oz. skein).

NOSE - Chain 78 st, turn. Row 1: Sc in ea ch, 2nd ch from hook through ch 38; in ch 39 sc 3 times; sc in ea ch from 40 through 77. Ch 1, turn. Row 2: Sc in ea sc of row 1; ch 1, turn. Row 3: Sc in ea sc of row 2 through st 39; in st 40 sc 3 times; sc to end of row; ch 1, turn. Row 4: Sc to end of row, ch 1, turn. Row 5: Sc in st 1 through 36, ch 6, sc in st 46 to end of row; ch 1, turn. Nose completed (adjust this to fit individual nose; if nose hole is too large, nose will "fall through" and mask will ride up into eyelashes -- very irritating!). Row 6: Sc in ea st of prev. row; ch 1, turn. Row 7: Sc in ea st of prev. row except dec 1 st between sts 3 and 4 of undernose section. Row 8: Dec 1 st at beginning and end of row, sc the rest. Rows 9 and 10: Sc to end; ch 1, turn. Row 11: Dec 1 st beginning and end, sc rest. Row 12: Sc to end; break off.

CHIN - Centering under nose section, attach yarn ; sc in 3 st of previous row; ch 1, turn. Row 14: Incr by 2 at beginning and end, sc between; ch 1, turn. Rows 15-22: Sc to end; ch 1, turn; except, incr by 1 st at beginning and end of rows 15, 17 and 21. After row 22, break off.

NECK - Using a blunt ended needle, whip edges of chin piece evenly to both sides of face portion; break off. Row 23: Attach yarn to face portion about 6 st from where chin joins; sc across chin section to an equal distance on other side; dec 2 st where junction occurs on both sides. Continue 5-7 more rows, gradually extending the rows out toward ends about 4 st at a time and dec in junction area as necessary to avoid bulkiness and give a smooth fit. Finish with a row which runs the whole length. Finish back closure with Velcro.

-- Excerpts from "Crocheted Face Mask,"
Signpost Bulletin No. 11

DETACHABLE SLEEVES - A down sweater with detachable sleeves
is useful. The sleeves can be removed and placed on the feet for
cold nights in a not-warm-enough sleeping bag.

DOUBLE-DUTY PAJAMAS - In keeping with the plan of making
one item serve more than one purpose, flannel pajamas can double as long underwear. Feet can be added to the pajamas, if desired, or a piece of elastic can be sewed on to fit under the instep to keep the pajama legs from sliding up.

WASHING DOWN JACKETS - I just finished hand washing my
down jacket. I put it in the washing machine for spin cycle only
to get the excess water out. Remember to handle garment very
carefully. Then I put it in the drier on warm; every 10-15 minutes I took it out and gently ruffled the clumps of down. Sure
enough, they de-matted and it looks like it's going to turn out
beautifully. Before anyone does it, though, I suggest they read
some instructions such as those in the REI catalog or in "Backpacking One Step at a Time."

MENDING - It's hard to believe, but I've found that Scotch tape
works for mending holes in down-filled nylon garments. I've got
a jacket that leaked down through a hole; I covered the hole up
temporarily with Scotch tape, which kept the down in all right.
And then the tape stuck on there even through washings. It's still
there, still mending the hole temporarily.

BUTTONS ON LEDERHOSEN - To replace buttons on alpine style
leather shorts, use gray shoestrings. Cut off the desired length
and tie the button onto the lederhosen with the knot on the inside.
This is much easier than trying to sew worn leather strips.

WATERPROOFING WOOL - Spraying a water repellent over wool
pants works pretty well. Wash the trousers only when really necessary; then re-apply the water repellent compound.

RAIN GARB ══

STAY DRY - If you get wet you are likely to get cold. Wet
clothing is much poorer insulation than dry clothing. The combination of cold, wet and windy is especially dangerous (even
when "cold" is above freezing). Carry a parka, anorak or poncho
and wear clothing (such as wool) which is warm even when wet.
Down-filled clothing must be kept dry to be effective insulation.

WET HIKING - A cagoule or poncho, used with rain pants, provides very good protection when ambling through a rain or crashing through dripping underbrush, but their tendency to hold moisture in as well as keep it out puts a limit on how hard you can hike. Build up a good sweat with a cagoule on and you will literally steam the insulative value out of your clothing.

When conditions are not so wet, a parka treated with a good water repellent will let your moisture escape while still keeping out mists, light rains or splatterings from the underbrush. As a durable treatment, we have found that spray repellents are not too effective. Most hardware stores carry water repellent solutions in bulk quantities, usually in pint or gallon cans. Saturate the garment in the solution and let it dry for several days. An average parka will soak up about a pint of solution, and cotton or cotton mix fabrics accept the treatment far better than synthetic materials. The smell of the solvent will probably persist for over a week, but then it fades away. The treatment will greatly decrease the amount of water the garment will absorb and will mean a shorter drying time when it does get wet.

Clothing, especially hat, shirt and pants, should preferably be of wool since it retains its insulative value even when wet. Pants could be treated with water repellent, but since they are likely to be washed much more frequently than a parka and since the repellent will not survive the soap, it might not be the most economical system. Some people rub wax into their pants on the front of the legs over the thighs and behind the legs over the calf, since those are the two parts that get wettest when hiking in rain.

-- Excerpts from an article, "Wet Hiking,"
by Rick Ells

PACK COVERING PONCHO - Take a standard store-bought poncho and cut apart across, behind the hood, halfway between the front and back halves of the upper set of snaps. Insert 32" (or however much it takes to go up and over your pack) of 55" width coated nylon and coat seams with seam cement. Form a casing on each side of the insert by turning over the selvage edges and stitching. At the back, fasten one end of a nylon rope and run it through the casing for a drawstring. At the front put a toggle. Put poncho on over pack, adjust sides with ropes and toggles to take up slack, snap snaps and go.

Other handy hints: Sew loops of nylon tape to corners of poncho, for use when tying poncho up as shelter. When sewing poly-coated nylon, use a roller-type presser foot to prevent grabbing and seam misalignment.

BLOWING PONCHO - A large flowing poncho tends to billow up like a spinnaker when there is any wind. This billowing can be prevented by a cord tied around the waist. Or by wearing the poncho under the pack.

IMPROVED CAGOULE - The cagoule, a full-length pullover rain
jacket, is a very useful piece of protective clothing particularly
in a wind driven rain. But its length, down to the boot tops for
most hikers, can restrict the stride. One solution is to permanently shorten the cagoule to knee length, but frequently the extra length comes in handy. Making the length adjustable is a
better method. Sew two tabs to the bottom hem of the cagoule
and two buttons to the inside seams about a foot below the arm-
pits. Then the cagoule can be either worn full length for just
standing around in the rain, or shortened for really stretching out
the stride when one wants to cover distance. A pair of rain chaps,
easily made at home, can be worn to protect the legs when the
cagoule is in its shortened position.

WATERPROOF TEST - To test for waterproofness of cloth, try to
breathe or blow through it.

IMPROVING RAIN GEAR - We have purchased the REI children's rain suits and found that modifications were in order. The
rainsuit uses a bib and suspenders. For young children this is a
terrible bother when they have to go to the bathroom, particularly if it is raining heavily. It means that they need help, taking off their jackets or getting the suspenders out from under the
jackets and then back up over again. We ended up cutting the
bibs off, discarding the suspenders, and either installing an
elastic waistband or a drawstring.
    Also, we put zippers along the outside of the rain pants
from the cuff to just above the knee to allow them to remove
and replace their pants without having to take off their boots.
Children tend to splash more and it is not recommended that the
zippers be placed on the inside of their rainpants. This did not
seem to be a particular problem for us adults.
    On our rain pants we put 22" zippers on the insides of the
legs. Not only could we remove and replace the pants easily
without removing our boots, but we could unzip them for ventilation when it was warm. By having the zippers on the inside,
we were less likely to get wet from contacting the brush as we
walked. Also, the wind was less likely to blow the rain against
our pants underneath.
    We put a snap fastener at the cuff so we could snap them
together at the bottom and still zip them open above. Having
them totally wide open however, even unsnapped, did not annoy
us in walking. The pants did not tend to flap against each other
or catch, as we had feared when we put the zippers on the inside
instead of the outside.
    Similar 22" zippers were placed in our hiking pants. This
not only allowed us to take them off and on without having to
remove our boots, but permitted the pants to be unzipped then
folded upward and attached by Velcro or belt loops to the upper
part of the pants or to the belt. Thus they could be immediately converted to shorts.

TWO-HEADED PONCHO - I invented a two-headed poncho to give rain protection to our little son when he rides in a Gerry Pack. The small head is about 3/4 the size of the large and is made just like it. Spacing is 10" between the back of my hood and the front of the other. If the distance is too short, the child will always be pulled forward. If too long, the fabric between hoods will sag and collect water. The child's hood must have a lip at the chin or water will run inside. When the poncho is used by an adult only, Velcro tabs hold the second hood under a flap.

PONCHO DRAINAGE - The ideal hiking poncho has not yet been invented, but apparently some individuals are making gradual improvements. One person told of seeing a hiker who had turned up the front bottom edge of his poncho about 6" and sewed it in place (or fastened it somehow). When it rained, the water ran down the front of the poncho, gathered in the 6" pocket, and then ran out the corners instead of off the front and down onto his boots.

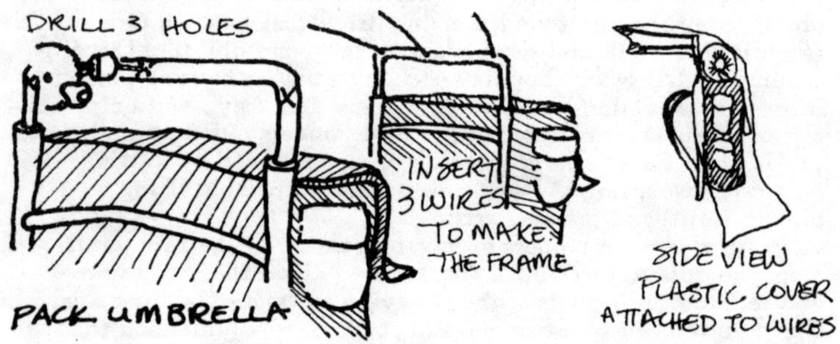

UMBRELLA - One way to beat the rain while hiking is to have an umbrella built into your backpack. One was devised by a Signposter using coated lightweight nylon and fiberglass tips from three old fishing rods. The fabric should be large enough to drape over your pack in the back and come to a shallow point in the center front to form, along with the front corners, three tips of an umbrella. Three holes were drilled in the pack frame -- one on each side and one in the center of the top. The holes angle outward so that when the fiberglass rods are in place they have to bend slightly to fit into the umbrella pockets at the three tips. The bending keeps the nylon taut above your head. An earlier version had longer sides to keep his arms dry, but this proved too cumbersome. (Ed. Note: Some beach hikers simply fasten a regular umbrella to their pack frame with a C-clamp.)

DOWN VS. SYNTHETICS - In the mountain shops of the Pacific
Northwest a strange thing has been happening: Down jackets and
sleeping bags are slowly being pushed off the shelves by products
using synthetic insulations. Not that down's day is past. Down is
still king of insulators -- lighter than a fluffy feather, able to be
compressed into a tiny stuff bag, and more expensive than a hard
week's wages. It's just that the synthetics industry is finally
coming up with products that are not only cheap but also good,
at least able to meet the needs of the average hiker.

A big selling point of synthetics is reliability. Let's say
that you and your buddy are fording a stream somewhere back in
the sticks. He has a Fiberfill II sleeping bag and you have a
down bag. You try to balance yourself on a slimy rock in mid-
stream and, whoosh! Both you and your buddy go down into the
icy waters. In your floundering about, you both manage to soak
your sleeping bags thoroughly, among other things. For your
buddy the job of restoring the insulative value of his sleeping
bag is as simple as squeezing it out and hanging it up to dry during a lunch break. His bag will still be damp, but because the
Dacron fibers absorb very little moisture, the bag will be able to
keep him reasonably warm.

For you, however, the job is a little more difficult. Down,
particularly new down, resists getting wet, but with persistence
it can be soaked well enough to absorb quite a bit of water.
Once wet, it loses almost all of its insulative value and, worse,
can take as much as a week to dry out enough to warm you again.
For you, the rest of the hike is going to be a little chilly at night.

Bags made with polyester insulation (like Dacron Fiberfill II
or PolarGuard) are cheaper. Well-made polyester fill sleeping
bags range in price from $35-$65, while down bags go from $65
on up to more than $150. However, synthetic fill bags are heav-
ier, ranging in weight from 4-1/2 to 5-1/4 pounds compared with
the 3-1/2 to 4-1/2 pounds of equivalent down bags. Also, they
are 20-40% bulkier than down bags when packed into their stuff
bags. Compressor bags can narrow the margin, but not much.

An extra pound or so and a little bulk seems a reasonable
load to carry if it means saving $50, but are the bags warm
enough? Any temperature rating of a bag is tenuous. Individual
differences in metabolism, physical condition and energy re-
serves, not to mention differences in the effectiveness of your
shelter, play a big role in determining whether you sleep comfy
and warm or shivering and miserable. The people Signpost
talked with -- including salesmen, guides and equipment design-
ers -- felt that if properly designed and used with proper shelter
and a ground mat the bags were good at least down to freezing.
For many people they would serve for as much as 10° colder.

> -- Excerpts from an article, "A Synthetic Goose?"
> by Rick Ells

SLEEPING BAGS FOR KIDS - The down bags in kiddy-size are
substantially more expensive than Dacron. Before buying the
down, make sure your child can live and breathe near down. An
allergy might demand Dacron from the start, and save you money.

DON'T OVER-BAG - When buying a sleeping bag, it's best to get
the least amount of bag you can get by with. You can always
add extra clothing or insulated sleepers if you only use it once a
year in really cold weather. No point in paying for or carrying
more down than you usually need.

ALL SEASONS BAG - With only one sleeping bag I often find
myself either too hot or too cold. Well, I have found a solution. A High & Light UNO-20 bag and a PLUS-12 liner. The
UNO-20 bag has a 2" thick, 7-foot polyurethane foam pad in
an egg crate design for a bottom and 22 ozs. prime goose down
on top. The temperature range goes down to zero and up to
about 50°. The PLUS-12 liner extends the temperature range by
about 20° with 12 ozs. of down. On those cold nights you can
combine the two, for warmer ones just use the bag, and for the
really warm ones just the liner.   This is truly a "bag for all
seasons." (Ed. Note: These same ideas are used in other brands
of sleeping bags, too.)

COZY SLEEP OUTFIT - My husband and I like sleeping together,
and that started us thinking how to be comfortable and warm and
carry minimum weight. We wanted 1-1/2" of foam pad to comfort our aging frames. Eliminating the down bag from underneath,
which compacts to negligible value anyway, reduced weight.
Our end product sleeps two, three in an emergency, with total
weight of 9-1/2 lbs.
    I made extra-long pillowcase covers for two 24x72" polyur-
ethane pads, coated nylon for the bottoms and lighter weight on
top. The extra length at the top end covers the pads when rolled;
tie cords are also attached. Being open, covers can easily be removed for washing. A 72" separating zipper sewed to opposite
sides of the two covers permits attaching them to form a double
pad, the bottom of our sleep outfit. The top is one opened out,
down sleeping bag -- attached to the pads by means of a 96" separating zipper sewed half to each pad cover, across the bottoms
and up the outside edges. (When buying this zipper be sure it
mates with the one on the sleeping bag. I got mine where we
bought the bag.)
    To assemble the outfit, place covered pads on groundcloth,
zip together, fluff sleeping bag and zip on top. This arrangement
has one disadvantage -- no hoods. To keep a warm head I wear
a wool hat and may even drape a wool sweater or such around my
shoulders in really cold weather. The warm, pleasant contact of
my husband nearby more than compensates for this inconvenience.
    The outfit carries easily in three stuff bags, two for the pads
and one for the sleeping bag.

THIN SPOTS - To examine a sleeping bag, stand up and put the bag on over your head. In a brightly-lighted room, look around for any thin spots or air spaces. These thin spots are where heat will escape. Obviously, you don't want any such flaws.

WARMER BAGS - The kind of sleeping bags with no zippers are warmer, and they are not nearly as hard to get into and out of as you might imagine.

BETTER INSULATION - A gimmick for increasing the warmth factor of sleeping equipment is to keep as much of the body out of direct contact with the underlying part of the sleeping bag as possible. The warmest position is lying on one's side with only a shoulder and hip touching the bottom of the bag. The feet may be elevated on a pack for additional warmth. Sometimes winter hikers put socks under the hip and shoulder for added insulation.

FOIL SNAGGING ZIPPER - Exasperated by a zipper that grabs your sleeping bag fabric and comes to a stubborn halt? Make sure your next bag has an anti-snag tape. The tape is sewed on the side of the zipper opposite the baffle -- 2" nylon webbing is sometimes used. It can be sewed on one edge only, or tack the other edge to the inner lining.

WASHING PROBLEM - My first experience with washing a down sleeping bag was a near disaster. The problem was air trapped inside -- it won't come out through wet nylon. Two ideas I plan to try the next time: 1) Soak the bag while it is tightly rolled, then dump it into the tub and unroll it in the water. 2) Keep the zipper closed at all times if there is air in the bag. The air inside the bag balloons the space between the inner and outer shells. It doesn't take much pressure there to rip the baffles. REI Co-op advised that repair of ripped baffles is not worth the cost. I did it myself and spent seven hours repairing three baffles. At least, the bag is clean!

SPECIAL SOAP FOR DOWN - "Fluffy" is the name of a special compound made by Edelrid (West Germany) for washing down sleeping bags and parkas and the like. They have it in the sleeping bag department at REI Co-op at $2. 95, which seems high until you compare it with the investment you have already in the down equipment. Also, Fluffy is a good buy when you consider the results. It has superior washing ability, gets the item really clean, and gives it loft like new -- or better! Another advantage, say those who've used it, is that this soap doesn't destroy the natural oils in the down, and it's these natural oils which keep the down lively and able to fluff up.

LAUNDERING DOWN - One Signposter tells us: I have washed
our down bags at least half a dozen times apiece and never had
a bad experience. First recommendation: Before you wash the
bag, check all the seams THOROUGHLY, particularly the stitching lines that hold the baffles on the inside. If you habitually
fold your bag the same way and roll it the same way before you
put it into the stuff sack, you get tremendous abrasion on the
stitching and this will cause the baffles to go out. If you see any
weak stitching do your best to reinforce it before you start.

To wash your bag: Go to a laundromat with one of those
huge washers that will take a 9x12 cotton rug. Preferably, the
machine should rotate a few times in one direction and then reverse and rotate a few times in the other direction. This action
is much more gentle, and the rinsing is much more thorough on
these machines than other kinds.

It's better to put two bags at a time in one of these big machines, along with at least one or two pairs of large tennis shoes.
The shoes are there to beat the air out of the bags and out of the
down, because the down will never get wet and wash otherwise.
For soap, use Ivory Snow and dissolve it in hot water before
pouring it into the machine.

Let the bags go through one complete cycle, then inspect
them. If they are still dirty, you left them too long before you
washed them in the first place. Put them through a second cycle.
As you watch your bag going round and round, if it looks like it's
not wetting all the way through -- if it looks like it still has dry
spots in it -- the same solution applies. Put it through again.

Then take your bag out and inspect it carefully once more
to make sure you haven't acquired any rips. If you have, you'll
lose all your feathers in the drier.

Hopefully you've gone to a laundromat that has a centrifu-
gal extractor. Put your bags, somewhat wadded up and preferably accordion-style, around the wall of the extractor. Make
sure there's slack in them, so that when they're stretched out on
the outside of the extractor the stitching won't break. Extract
most of the water.

Then put your bags into a dryer at low or medium low heat.
Put the tennis shoes into the dryer with them; they will help to
break up the knots of down so it can dry thoroughly. Check with
your hand on the dryer door several times to make sure the bag
is not getting overheated. Dry your bags very well. They
should not be more than just slightly damp, and there should be
no knots of down in them. If, as they're drying, you find knots
break them open by massaging them with your hands. Then put
the bags back and dry some more. When you get home, just to
make sure, hang them up in a good airy place and let them dry
some more.

At all times while you're washing and drying your bags,
watch the machines for signs of feathers. If you should see any
feathers showing, stop the machine IMMEDIATELY, take out
your bag and sew it up, or you will lose them all and the laundromat owner will despise you. The feathers clog his filters and
cause all kinds of horrible problems.

DRYING SLEEPING BAGS - Some mildewy sleeping bags were
hung on the line all day and all night to freshen them. But, alas,
it rained. The owner phoned the cleaners for advice. They said
not to put the sleeping bags in the dryer, but still they wouldn't
take them wet. The owner knew that kapok can't go into the
dryer but Dacron can, and that's what these bags were.

The average home dryer is not big enough to properly tum-
ble such a big item, but our heroine was worried that if she took
the bags to the local laundromat the dryer setting would not be
low enough. So, she dried the bags at home. She put the dryer
on the lowest heat, then ran it for five minutes with the sleeping
bags in it, then opened the machine and took out the contents
and shifted them around. Then she ran it for another five minutes. Then she gave the bags a rest and repeated the 10-minute
drying process another time. Worked fine. She let them finish
drying stuffed with crumpled paper.

ZIPPERS - Some observers say that any kind of zipper with great
huge teeth grabs up hunks of cloth LESS than those with little
teeth. Also they work easier. Those with smoothly rounded
metal or, even better, plastic teeth snag less than those with
sharp edges. Aluminum teeth are worse than brass or plastic.

DOUBLE STUFF SACK - To guarantee a dry sleeping bag each
night, make a double waterproof stuff sack. Stuff the bag into
one sack. Then, slip that sack, open end first, into another one.

STUFFING YOUR SACK - If you have a pad to sleep on, roll it
up and pack it into the stuff bag first. Then stuff the sleeping
bag into the space that's left. They'll both fit this way.

STUFF BAG CAPACITY -- Inside the usual miniature duffel bag
type stuff bag, the following items can easily be carried: A 2-
pound McKinley down sleeping bag; a Dacron-insulated sleepsuit
which can also be worn around camp; wool stocking cap; shorty
air mattress (dust inside with talcum powder to prevent sticking).

SPACE BLANKETS - These are better than plastic for waterproofing but not really good as insulation on cold ground -- though
slightly warmer than plastic. I sleep under a plastic tarp and on
the edge of a space blanket, with part thrown over me. Used the
blanket in winter at Lake Wenatchee with my old Army down bag
on top. Woke up in the morning feeling warm and cozy, but my
skin was cold. (I used to get cold real easy outdoors, so started a
cold-shower-in-the-morning habit. Now I stand the cold well.)
I never use an insulating pad when packing in -- like going light.

EMERGENCY BAG COVER - Always carry a plastic bag large
enough to hold your sleeping bag. Don't count on your waterproof stuff sack to keep your bag completely dry if rain starts
while you're on the trail.

THERM-A-REST - This is an insulated air mattress, polyurethane in a coated nylon case. It is 19x47" in size, weighs about
1-1/2 lbs., priced at about $27. One friend has one and says he
slept like a baby for the first time on a backpack; the Therm-a-
Rest made all the difference in the world. It's available at REI
Co-op, Eddie Bauer, and elsewhere. Another friend who has one
reports that a Blue-Foam pad is wider and longer and one pound
lighter. Ensolite is the same weight. But the Therm-a-Rest is
VERY comfortable.

END SLIPPING - Since the Therm-a-Rest has a nylon cover and
many sleeping bags also have a nylon cover, the combination is
very slippery and you can easily slip off the mattress. REI has a
remedy for that. It's called "Tennis-goo." Yep! It's a rubber
compound for repairing tennis shoes. But if you apply it in strips
on the nylon Therm-a-Rest cover and let it dry thoroughly, it
will become a rubbery, non-slippery material that provides just
the right amount of holding power.

ENSOLITE - In summer, 1/4" thickness is sufficient; but 3/8" is
better for winter camping.

NEW AIR MATTRESS - With backpacking gaining popularity, a
multitude of new products are now on the market. One of these
is the Air Lift mattress. What makes this so different is that each
of its nine air tubes is separate. The mattress is held together by
a shell of rip stop nylon taffeta that zips closed to protect the
tubes. Included with the mattress are a nylon stuff bag, an extra
tube and a patch kit.

AIR-DOWN MATTRESS - Can this idea be true? Take a medium quality air mattress, tear apart the seams, shoot some down
into it, and close the seams back up. You then inflate it and
have a nice warm winterized air mattress.

*

OLD IDEA - A reader responded: The down-filled air mattress
idea is an old one. It was last popular about 15 years ago, when
it was replaced by the much more efficient Ensolite. Down-
filled air mattresses cannot ever be blown up by mouth, since
moisture in breath would soon mat the down. Those who used
this concept always carried a foot pump inflator.

TENTS AND TARPS - The choice of tent depends on several factors such as price, weight, area in which it will be used, frequency of use, and personal desires. Most popular for backpacking are two-man tents that come in hundreds of shapes, styles, weights, materials and prices. Your needs will vary from mine.

A tent is made up of a number of parts; each must do its job. The floor should be of waterproof material that will keep all water out and not puncture easily. It should come up several inches on the sides and ends, forming a watertight box. This keeps the occupants dry and eliminates the need for wilderness-damaging tent ditching.

The roof should be water resistant enough to withstand the hardest rain. The ends should have adequate screened ventilation to prevent condensation and to cool the tent in warm weather without letting the bugs in. I like fully zippered closures for the entrance.

Condensation is a major problem in some climates. During the night condensation can total a quart of water and ventilation cannot control this fully. The most satisfactory solution seems to be a double roof. The roof of the tent should be of breathable material which will allow the moisture-laden air to pass through it. Above this a completely waterproof fly is used. Condensation takes place on the underside of the fly and runs down to drip on the ground instead of in the tent. In very cold weather a frost liner of absorbent material can be used to prevent condensation.

The easier a tent is to erect and the fewer stakes and cords needed, the better. Shock cords for all lines will lengthen tent life by reducing the amount of stress on the tent material caused by wind flapping. A tent that is well sewed and made of quality material will give you long service, if properly cared for.

For the backpacking novice, the plastic tarp is often the only financially feasible way to go. This can be a plastic tube tent, plastic tarp, or coated cloth which is usually nylon. The tube tent is a cylinder of 3-mil plastic, about 9' long, that can be hung on a line to form a tent-like structure for sleeping. It is lightweight and inexpensive, but it tears easily and has very limited life. For the regular user it would become expensive tentage in time.

A more popular item is a 9x12', 4-mil plastic sheet (I prefer 6-mil for longer life). With 10 grommets, which you can easily install, this versatile shelter can be erected in many ways. A few simple rules: 1) Rig it close to the ground if wind is a factor. You may need to anchor edges with logs or rocks. 2) Use shock cords on your lines to minimize wind flapping. 3) Protect it when packing so it will not be punctured. Do not use it for a ground cloth as this can also put holes in it.

-- Excerpts from "Tent and Tarp Shelters," Signpost
Bulletin No. 8, by Brad Bradley

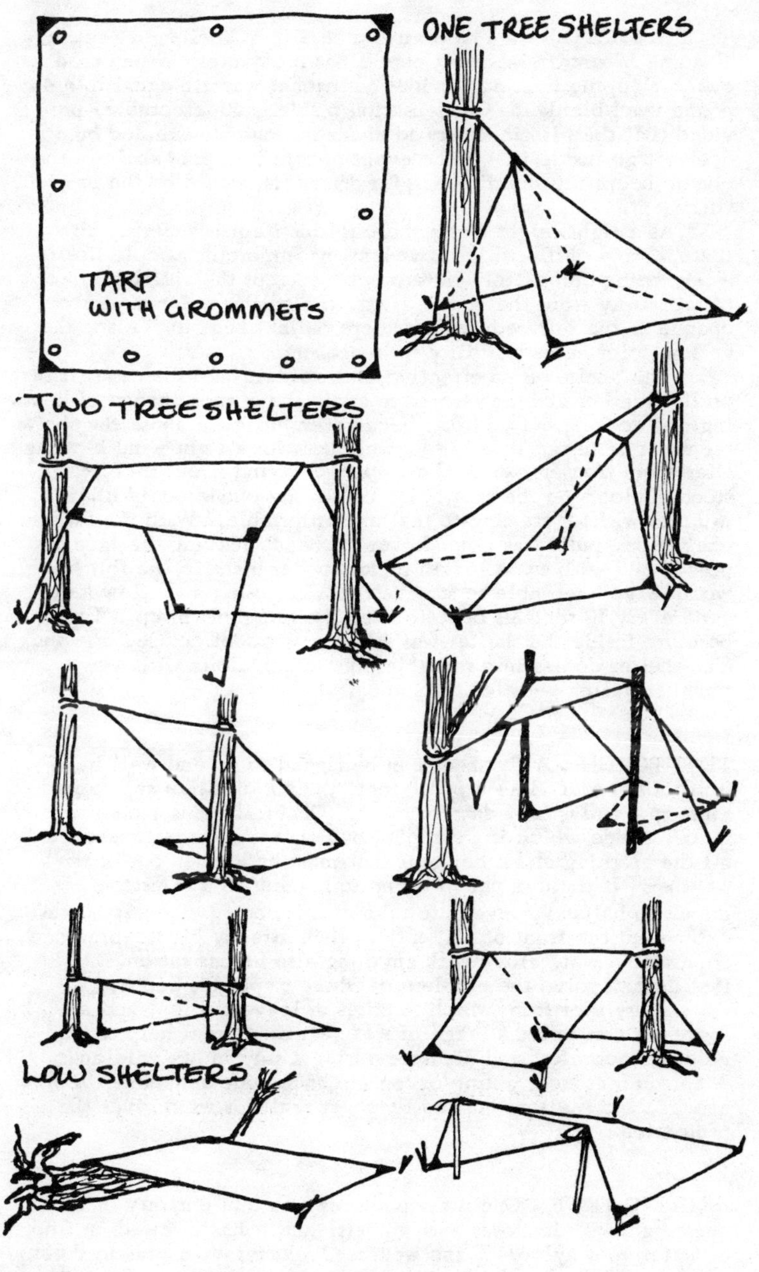

TARP WITH GROMMETS
ONE TREE SHELTERS
TWO TREE SHELTERS
LOW SHELTERS

STORM SHELTER - The plastic tube Storm-Shelter put out by
Tacoma Mountain Rescue Council has many uses. When used
over a sleeping bag, it provides additional warmth equal to a 4-
pound wool blanket. Condensation inside is undetectable, provided that the plastic is tucked under the chin so exhaled breath
does not go inside it. In the event of rain in a poor shelter, the
plastic keeps the sleeping bag far drier than would be the case
without it.

As a lightweight storm shelter, this item is superb. First,
it stops wind chill, which is at least as important as cold itself.
Next, being completely waterproof, it keeps the chilling effect
of rain away from the body. Next, the yellow color is partly
opaque to the infrared, which keeps radiant heat in. Also, the
yellow color helps visibility for searchers.

This shelter is so effective that at least one hiker uses it in
chilly weather at lunch stops, to avoid the abrupt change of heat-
ing and cooling. This hiker became enthusiastic about the shelter when he tested it in 13° F. weather with a light wind blowing.
Dressed in trousers, dress shirt, sport coat and street shoes, he
stood outdoors on the snow. He could stay outside only 10-15
minutes without starting to feel uncomfortable. With the Storm-
Shelter on, pulled as a hood over his head, leaving the face exposed, and with extra length tucked under his feet, he felt he
would have been able to survive the night using a shallow knee
bend every 10 seconds or so to keep the metabolism up. Temperature inside the shelter was 40° F., with, of course, no wind.
The shelter comes in a reusable plastic bag along with a two-
toned signaling whistle; costs about $1.

TENT PORCH - A fly sheet can be rigged to extend well in
front of the tent, like a porch roof. Think of a tent set up in
some spot to last 3-4 days or more. Generally it is a confined
space, inside which is a sleeping bag or two and mattresses, and
all the clothing and other gear that must be kept in out of the
weather. If the camper walks up to his tent in a rainstorm,
crawls in halfway, inverts to take off his boots (which, of course,
extend out the front of his tent) -- then already his sleeping bag
is partially wet, along with anything else he has sat on. And
that doesn't solve the problem of where to put his boots.

A dry spot from which to enter or leave the tent and a
space for controlled storage of wet gear offers real help toward
achieving comfort and pleasure during a stay in our wildlands.
A convenient tree, stump or log might provide assistance in creating such a shelter, but the fly sheet really is what gives the
protection.

NETTING TENT - One man made his own tent entirely of mos-
quito netting. It closes with zippers, and it has a sewed-in floor
of waterproof nylon. If the weather looks rainy, a plastic sheet
can be thrown over the tent.

TENT WINDOWS - For more light inside a tent, those who do not fear ruining their tent might install clear plastic windows. One backpacker has added four to his 2-man mountain tent.

TUBE TENTS - They look good but don't work out as well as expected, at least not in damp climates. They get wet on the inside from the condensation of body vapors, and they are cramped so that it is impossible to keep sleeping bag or clothing dry. For those who do use a tube tent, the following suggestions are made: 1) Don't use a black one as it shows dirt too easily and the interior is worse than a cave. Do use a clear one or an orange one. 2) When erecting the tube tent, use two cords through the tent for the ridge line. Make two spreader bars from dowels about 8-10" long and notch the ends. Inserting these at each end to spread the cords will give a narrow flat roof. Now there is sit-up room. The use of spreader bars will also eliminate just about all of the moisture condensation. 3) Carry a few spring clothes-pins. After climbing into the sack, snap together excess plastic along the ground at the ends to create a turned-up sill. The sill seems to discourage 4-footed furry creatures from exploring in your tent and also helps prevent water from running through it in case of a downpour. 4) If a tarp suits the night better, slit the tube and rig it as a tarp.

PLASTIC TARPS - More maneuverable than tube tents are the 9x9' or larger tarps of 4-mil plastic. With six Visklamps or grommet tapes and several lengths of nylon cord, several styles of rigging may be used, providing serviceable roof and room at minimum expense and weight until such time as the hiker is ready to invest in a real tent. A 2-mil sheet of plastic can be used for a ground cloth.

ON TARPS - Results of a discussion on the merits of tarps: A tarp is adequate most of the time in the Cascades, except when you need a tent.

NIGHT-TIME CONSTRUCTION - A hiker described a time when he had to put his shelter up in the dark. "Something went wrong," he says. "Shortly after it began to rain, when I wiggled my toes I could hear water splashing." . . That was not one of his best nights. Since then he's made a rule of putting the shelter up before dark.

EMERGENCY SHELTER - A couple of heavy duty king-size garbage bags can provide cheap but effective emergency protection. Pull one over your head, the other over your legs. Punch a few air holes. You are protected from heat loss due to direct contact of water on your skin.

SPACIOUS SHELTER - The rainfly of a Mount McKinley tent can
be used as a shelter by itself. It is conical in shape, held up by
an 88" center pole, and fastened down with ties all around. It
clears the ground about a foot and provides a roof over an area
approximately 8x8' with enough headroom to stand up. It is
adaptable to use as a bath house too. The fly weighs 2-1/4
pounds and the pole 1-1/2 pounds.

PRACTICE - Hikers new to backpacking will find problems
enough as they master unaccustomed skills. Some have found it
wise to set up their tent or tarp at home, at least once before
trying to do it in strange surroundings when they are tired and
wet and a strong wind is blowing. Another suggestion from accomplished backpackers is to cook a couple of meals at home
just as you plan to do on the trail. Sure saves on disappointment
out in the wilderness.

TENT PEGS IN SNOW - To hold your tent pegs when setting up
camp on snow: Drill holes through both ends of the peg, run ends
of a cord through the holes, knot each end so it won't pull back
through. Make an overhand knot at the center of the cord to
form a loop above the peg. Lay peg in a snow trench about 6"
deep and bury. Fasten tent cord to exposed loop. Under most
conditions this will not pull out. Red avalanche cord is easiest to
see when pulling out the pegs.

GRAVEL CAMPING - If you have to camp on gravel and you are
feeling unhappy about it, consider these advantages: 1) Rain
soaks into the gravel so you don't have water standing around the
tent. 2) No matter how hard it rains, gravel never turns to mud.
3) Gravel doesn't blow into your food or track into your bedding
unless it is very fine. Then it is called "sand." 4) Gravel is
not the natural habitat of mosquitoes, chiggers or ticks.

MAKESHIFT GROMMETS - To tie out a plastic tarp, use a handful of dirt wadded into a ball and wrap the corner of the tarp
around it. Tie a string around the lump, and you're ready to
fasten the tarp to anything.

MEMORY - When training Scouts or any other young people to
construct a shelter correctly, the instructor eventually "gets to
them," but not the first time out. The youngsters have to get
good and wet first before they remember.

HIGHLIGHTING MAPS - Since trail lines on topographic maps
are not readily visible, highlight them with transparent ink in a
felt point marking pen. Sometimes a magnifying glass is needed
to help in this job.

WHERE TO GO - Many persons subscribe to Signpost so they can
get ideas on places to go. Another way to get ideas is to get
acquainted with your local public library. Find out what guide-
books they have on the shelves or can borrow for you. They will
be on climbing, paddling, bicycling, as well as trail travel.

   If you need to use a guidebook often, perhaps you should try
to buy copies of those you find useful. Try a secondhand store
first. Cut out the pages you need and take them on whatever trip
you make. When you return, slip the page back into its place.
Put a rubber band around the book to keep everything together.
Many hikers are observed on the trails with copies of an entire
guidebook in their hands. This is not only very hard on the book
but it must also be a nuisance to the hiker. It's YOUR book so
you can cut it apart if you want to. It's just a useful tool. Make
it serve you!

IDEAS FROM MAPS - Whether you take one trip or 20 in a year,
it's worthwhile to acquire some maps. You should have a recre-
ation map of each national forest or park you visit most often.
The other map useful for finding places to go is the topographic
quadrangle map, or "quad." Buy a few of these a year and
eventually you'll have a couple file drawers full. Pick a quad at
random and sit down and "read" it. How about that little lake
with no name there just above Lost Lake; do you think there is
really no trail to it when the contour intervals show gentle terrain
between them? What's that thing labeled "old railroad grade?"
It takes off from the road -- why not see if you can find it?
There's a bunch of contour lines all together. Bet that's a cliff
with a great view. You'll "see" a lot more once you start reading your maps for ideas.

OLD MAPS - An addition to the discussion on using maps as idea
sources for places to go: Old maps are valuable here, too. If
you don't happen to have old maps on hand, you can buy them.
A good assortment is one called Sportsman's (or Sportsman) Log,
available at most hunting shops. Often the single county maps
displayed for sale at the same stores are made from out-of-date
plates too. These maps don't show present roads, don't show
present trails, tend to indicate trails as simplified straight lines,
and often show trails as stopping abruptly at section lines. But if
you like to do trail detective work, spend a rainy afternoon stud-
ying them.

DECEPTIVE PACKAGING - Sporting goods stores may display
sets of maps in flashy, modern-looking packages. Because they
contain so many maps, they look like a good buy. Closer in-
spection may show that the maps are not dated. Usually a map
which is not dated should be suspect; even if it is obviously of
recent printing, the actual information can be 20 or so years old.

MAP MEASURER - Years ago I purchased a little device for running along maps to figure out how much mileage was involved
on certain trips. But I couldn't get it to work, so I returned it
and gradually developed a very accurate eye for estimating distances. But recently I had occasion to use a map measurer again
and this one is a fine precision instrument. It gave accurate results in much less time than my old "eyeballing" method. For
anyone who does much trip planning, this German-made device
(Kurvenmesser) is a real help. Mine comes from Eddie Bauer, is
priced under $5. It's in a protective case; this is not a kid's toy.

COMPASS STICKING - One of the things that can go wrong with
a compass, or can be wrong when you buy it, is that the needle
may not swing freely. Place your compass on a non-metallic
surface and clear of all possible magnetic interference. Move
the case, twisting it to the left and right. The needle should
remain pointing steadfastly northerly, toward the magnetic pole.
On some compasses the needle has been found to be off by many
degrees. Check yours now, before you need it.

UNUSUAL COMPASS PROBLEM - One member of a class in alpine
travel techniques was having trouble getting accurate compass
readings. In fact, she was having an extraordinary amount of
difficulty, with the compass as much as 20° off. They told her it
was metal interfering with the operation of the needle. Several
possible culprits were removed from the scene, but the lady finally discovered the cause of the malfunction. It was the wire in
her bra.

MUSLIN MOUNTING - For an easy-to-make waterproof perma-
nent mounting for maps, the following ingredients are needed:
a map, a piece of bleached muslin slightly larger than the map,
glue, acrylic spray or clear shellac spray. Attach the muslin to
a board. Cut the map on its fold lines and glue it to the muslin
leaving the width of a pencil between each piece of map. Let
the glue dry thoroughly and remove the muslin from the board.
Then spray both sides of the muslin. Result is one waterproof
map with no creases to cause blurring.

MAP COVERS - The plastic covers or protectors for golf club
handles are big enough to take one or two USGS quads tightly
rolled. Saves putting creases in those valuable maps. Get some
cheap ones and cut to length easily with a sharp knife.

PLASTIC SPRAY - Printing maps on waterproof paper is a great
idea, but an imitation can be made at home. Spraying paper
items with clear plastic makes them definitely water resistant,
although they will not withstand real soaking.

TRANSPARENT MYLAR - A strong transparent mylar laminate
can be applied over maps and trail descriptions to make them
more durable for outdoor use. The sheets are easy to apply and
bond permanently. They are not cheap (a 9x12" sheet is about
30¢) but can save an often-used map.

MARKERS ARE LITTER - Unless route marking tape is removed
by the group which applies it, it is litter the same as any other
debris abandoned in the hills. It is best to use it only in real
emergencies. The last person down should gather up the markers
as he or she descends.

COLORFUL MARKERS - Someone has discovered that the bright
colored, candy covered chocolate drops called M&M's make
good trail markers in snow. Their bright colors spread and are
easy to see.

TRAIL MARKERS - I was born in Puget Sound country and therefore do not often let the weather change my plans, but hike in
spite of it. I always carry topog maps, a very good compass, and
-- most important -- an altimeter. This latter is a vital aid in
fog or clouds when a compass sight cannot be used.
    Frequently I flag my routes in and remove flags outbound.
I have read recently of irate hikers removing tape flags they come
upon. I do know I have, on occasion, missed a tape or two on a
back trail on my way out, so a random piece of my old, weath-
ered tape could be picked up as litter sometimes.
    But my bad dream always involves my sons and myself miss-
ing a critical back trail because someone has removed our flags
and having to bivouac under very bad conditions, always on a
nasty steep mountain that I love, fear and respect. No mountain
man worth his weight in wet blueberry bushes would cut a rope on
a mountain before he knew whether someone hung on the end; so
why would he cut a flag line that someone may be on the other
end of?
    Flag removal bothers me for other reasons: We all hike on
land of various ownership, and flag lines are used for potential
trail and road routes, boundary lines, and timber management.
They are put in by the expenditure of money, either public or
private. To take flag lines out is not only potentially dangerous
but also stealing or vandalism.

LIGHTER PACK - A backpacker who can take off for a weekend in the mountains with a total load of about 12 lbs. must have really done some thinking. How can it be accomplished? One Sierra Mountains hiker takes only the following items: Pack, 21 ozs.; sleeping bag, 37 ozs.; 2x4' Ensolite pad, 8 ozs.; tarp and cord, 12 ozs.; flashlight, 4 ozs.; maps, 6 ozs.; camera, 20 ozs.; miscellany, 8 ozs.; down shirt, 22 ozs.; windbreaker, 8 ozs.; wind pants, 5 ozs.; extra socks, 3 ozs.; towel, 3 ozs.; pan and holder, 6 ozs.; cup and spoon, 4 ozs.; water bag, 2 ozs.; food.

Weight has been cut either by finding a lighter brand or by devising multi-purpose equipment. For example, the sleeping bag is one which the hiker made himself. On really cold nights, the down shirt supplements the sleeping bag. The Ensolite pad is minimal. The 2-mil plastic tarp (8x8') serves as ground cloth and shelter and in lieu of a poncho when folded in half and worn as a cape over pack and all. The camera gets twice the pictures per roll as the usual apparatus. The cooking pan is a rectangular loaf pan which can be set across a couple of rocks, requiring no grate. It fits snugly in a side pocket of the pack and is just large enough so that most of the food can be packed inside it.

The water bag doubles as a pillow later, when filled with air; originally it was the liner of a 2-1/2 gal. milk carton. It holds sufficient water for all the cooking chores of a small group and can even be used to carry water in a pack on dry trails (it neatly shapes itself to whatever space is available in the pack). The miscellaneous items include: The ever-important matches; emergency kit with ready bandages, moleskin, tape, aspirin, pencil and paper; and personal items including insect repellent, toothbrush and paper tissues.

With such a light load, no pack frame is required to support it, thus saving even more weight.

ARMY ISSUE FOR PACKING - Anyone who has access to surplus military equipment can utilize it quite nicely for recreational backpacking. That is, as long as its excessive sturdiness is not considered a drawback. Such an outfit was demonstrated for the Signpost staff a while back -- the Combat M-1956 field pack with the pistol belt, canteen and ammunition pouches. Not quite a Kelty, but it will carry a lot of gear.

PEACE AND QUIET - A squeaky pack frame is an annoyance to the wearer and to everyone else within earshot on the trail. The cure is simple -- merely lubricate the points of friction. From an auto supply house, obtain a stick of stainless lubricant (intended for use on car door latches, but also useful on home latches and wooden drawer runners). Unlace the pack frame back bands. Apply a generous layer of lubricant on the side rails and the inside of the bands, at the points where they come in contact. Replace the bands. Result: Peace and quiet!

DAY PACK - A belt-pouch which converts to a small frameless
day pack can be purchased for $3-$6. Most models seem to be
of nylon, with drawstring top covered by a rounded flap. Shoulder straps are adjustable but unpadded. To convert it the belt-
pouch is unzipped, turned inside out and shaken to loosen the
folds into pack shape. Handy for side trips, too.

RAINPROOF SEAMS - Merchandisers say that customers demand
coated fabrics and flap-covered zippers, even though the seams
of such packs or other items may leak. Perhaps it is pretty generally accepted that any item of cloth equipment is going to require a coating of a seam sealant.

PACK REPAIRS - A request from a reader who needed sewing repairs made on a pack led to the discovery that it is, indeed, possible to have fabrics repaired. Many outdoor equipment stores
have repair services for packs and tents. Some do it right on the
premises, although it probably would be too much to hope to get
it while you wait. Outfitters selling merchandise of their own
manufacture may provide free repairs. Check with the place you
purchased the item.

PACK STRAPS - New straps should be purchased for a pack before the old ones reach the dangerously worn stage. And the re-
placement should be made at home, not on the trail. Supply
stores carry such straps, complete with necessary padding,
grommets and buckles.

POCKETS - For packs that seem too small, the addition of outside pockets may relieve the situation. Pockets are for sale in
assorted sizes. The purchaser places and sews them on the pack
himself.

TINY BAGS - Plastic baby bottle fillers come in a long roll, like
supermarket produce bags. One end of each is already sealed.
When torn off the string, it becomes a very small, quite durable
bag (much heavier plastic than sandwich bags). Useful for packing small quantities of foods. Can be closed with rubberband or
twist of wire. They are about 3x7", flat, cost less than 2¢ each.

PLASTIC BAG USES - Waterproof plastic bags are available in
all sizes. Appropriate sizes can be used to protect rolled sleeping
bags, to cover packs while being worn or when set down, to hold
clean or soiled clothing, to wear as emergency rain shirts and
skirts, to pack out garbage, to protect dry firewood overnight, or
to cover the foot of a sleeping bag which sticks out from under a
crowded tarp.

BAGGING - Everything in a pack should be in its own plastic bag.
Keeps things neat, and (oh, boy!) dry. When a hiker stops on the
trail and rummages in the rain for a woolen cap, everything in
the pack gets rained on. Two or three days of this can be depress-
ing. Using plastic bags means that when the camper climbs into
his warm down bag at night his socks are dry, his sleepwear is dry,
his sweater is dry, and he can snuggle down and enjoy listening to
the raindrops on the tarp.

MORE USES - Use plastic bags for everything. Money, even --
a bag is lighter than a wallet. Plastic map case with zipper fits
the compartment on the back of my pack. Keep maps and little
flat things in it; you can pull it out, look through the plastic and
reach in to get what you want right away.

SLIPCOVER - A plastic garbage can liner makes a waterproof
slipcover for a pack which must stand outside a tent overnight.

LABEL POCKETS - Try placing strips of surgical adhesive tape
over the different pockets on your pack to label what's inside.
This method can save a good deal of searching time. Particularly, mark where your first aid kit is located.

QUICK ACCESS - Being able to lay hands on flashlight, map,
knife or bug repellent without delay can be almost as important
as the items themselves. Pockets help achieve this. So does
putting the things in the same spot each trip.

CUT COSTS - It's silly for anyone to pay 85¢ for a poly bottle,
when a quart Clorox bottle, washed out, will do just as well.
And you don't have to buy plastic tubes, either. Hair coloring
bottles, mustard and catsup squeeze bottles and plastic cheese
spread bottles hold butter, honey, peanut butter, and jam just as
well (tape the tops so they don't leak in your pack).

LAB EQUIPMENT - Some stores not oriented to backpacking are
nevertheless worth a visit or a catalog request. Scientific supply
houses may have departments for over-the-counter sales, and
their catalogs may be available there or at the local public library. Many of the products sold by such companies have their
principal backpacking applications as containers for liquids,
foods and first aid supplies. Some of the more useful or interest-
ing are: Polyethylene bottles, 1/2 to 32-oz. sizes; polyethylene
washing bottles, useful for dry camps; polyethylene dropping
bottles; rubber stoppers; polypropylene test tubes and caps;
and polyethylene vials with attached lids.

LIST - One of the basic questions to ask when selecting hiking
equipment: "Is it necessary?" The answer is not always clear.
For day hikes, the "ten essentials" may suffice. For longer hikes
it is harder to decide just what to carry. A good start is one of
the many good lists prepared from the experience of others, selecting from the optional items according to personal preference.
Keep a list of what was actually carried. The items on it will
change after each hike, as the list maker observes other hikers.
Without the list, one might forget the changes he wanted to
make, or necessary articles might be left at home. With a list,
the pack can be assembled faster and easier.

WEIGHT - One of the most deceptive phrases that a backpacker
can hear is, "It hardly weighs anything." It's unbelievable how
a pack filled with things that weigh practically nothing can reg-
ister 40 lbs. on the scales.

HIKING & CLIMBING GEAR

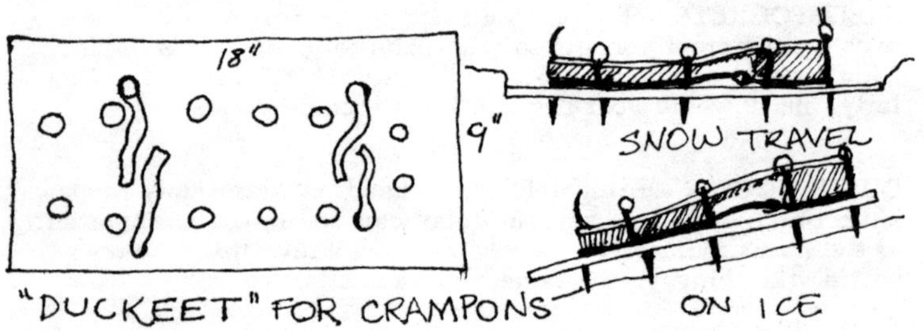

DUCKFEET FOR CRAMPONS - Climbers and hikers know the
problems of traveling on late winter and spring snow. Breaking
through a thin crust and floundering with every step is both tiring
and frustrating. Snowshoes and touring skis can be used to solve
the problem but they are heavy to carry on the approach to snow,
and they are tricky to use when on steep snow. Lightweight
"duckfeet" attached to the bottoms of crampons have proven
their worth on consolidated snow and made the first winter ascent
of Mount Mills (California) possible. Here's how to make your
own 12-oz. duckfeet as suggested by Bob Thomas, writing in
"The Roadrunner," publication of the Kern-Kaweah Chapter of
the Sierra Club.
    Cut two pieces of 3/16" plywood measuring 9x18" each and
smooth the rough edges. Cover with a single layer of fiberglass
for added strength. Drill holes to fit your crampon spikes, allowing the wood to fit flush against the bottoms. Drill more holes at
mid-toe and heel for nylon cord tie-ons. The protruding crampon spikes will provide traction. When the hiking or climbing
angle becomes too steep for the duckfeet, or when the snow is
firm enough for boots, just untie the cords and hang the lightweight feet on your pack.

ICE AXE CARRY - An elastic loop sewed on the back of a pack
near the top right provides a holder for an ice axe. The axe can
be slipped through the loop and can be tied at the bottom or held
by one of the sleeping bag straps. It is readily removed for action. . . Some people prefer to carry the ice axe horizontally,
tucked between pack and frame. For brief intervals it can be
rested across the shoulder straps, just behind the neck.

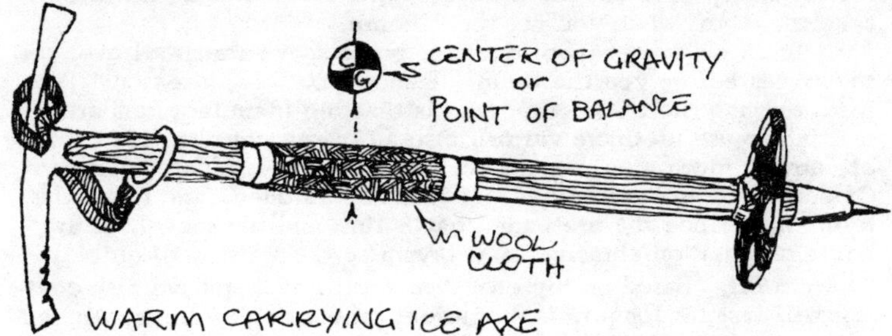

WARM CARRYING - If you frequently carry your metal ice axe
by the shaft, you can quickly locate the balance point and, at
the same time, keep your hand warmer on cool days by taping a
piece of wool cloth at that point. If you use a snow basket, remember to figure in its weight when finding the balance point.

SNOWSHOE HINTS - 1) Snowshoes can be carried in gentle terrain
by putting the pointed end of a ski pole or ice axe through the
toe holes and resting the pole on your shoulder with snowshoes
hanging behind. 2) Save money on antifog stick for your goggles.
Use a piece of Ivory soap. Rub the soap in a thin layer on the
inside surface of eyeglasses or goggles; then smooth out with fa-
cial tissue or handkerchief to an invisible coating.

3) You can make a comfortable seat in the snow using two
snowshoes. First, pack an area the size of one snowshoe while
you still have them both on. Then take them off and place one
on the packed area. Sink the other vertically behind it for a
backrest. Stamp a trench in front of the horizontal shoe for your
feet. An Ensolite pad to sit on completes the seat. 4) If you always dragged your feet as a child, it will probably help your
snowshoeing. A shuffling gait is a very efficient way of walking.
Pick up only the front of your snowshoe, thus lifting less weight.

5) A quick descent of a fairly steep, soft slope can be made
by running. Don't worry about falling. You will. Then you'll
know why a soft slope is required. 6) If a slope is steep enough,
"ski" down on snowshoes, either standing or sitting. Trail or
cross-country shoes without rope wrapping give best results. (This
trick is not for beginners. Sloping snow may avalanche easily,
and it takes considerable experience to judge this factor.)
7) And, don't forget to put sun protection cream on your ear lobes
and the undersides of your nose and chin.

-- Excerpts from an article, "Some Snowshoeing Hints
the Books Don't Tell You," by Graeme Blake

RAWHIDE SNOWSHOE CARE - Anybody who buys rawhide laced snowshoes is in for a lot of work. When people bring their badly beat-up snowshoes to me (author designs and builds snowshoes), I ask a good price to fix them; it takes about three times as long as weaving from scratch. You have good reason to do it yourself.

NEW SNOWSHOES - When you buy rawhide snowshoes don't let the salesperson put the bindings on. You will only have to take them off when you get them home.

Brush on two coats of exterior grade spar varnish all over the snowshoes before you use them. I know you want a reason: The word through the trade grapevine is that big manufacturers are starting to use urethane varnish instead of spar varnish; it's cheaper, covers more area per gallon, and requires less care to apply. Of course, it is waterproof -- if it isn't scratched, and that's the problem. Since the urethane coat is thin and the snowshoes are being dragged on abrasive snow crystals, the finish will quickly be worn off. Based on my own tests the thicker spar varnish coating will last far longer, is fungicidal preventing mold growth, and will extend the life of the snowshoes.

BOOTS - Many persons who bring relatively new snowshoes in for repair confess that they use Vibram soled boots. All I can say about that is "Don't!" They cause excessive wear on rawhide laces. Indians and Eskimos use soft soled moccasins and mukluks to protect their snowshoes.

I, personally, use full laced rubber pacs when I go out. They are cheaper than hiking boots. They don't get moldy like leather does. They stay dry and warm, and they have soles which cause only reasonable wear on snowshoes. I am thinking of getting another pair, grinding the soles flat, and then gluing felt on the bottoms to make rubber mukluks! Steelheaders do this to their waders. For years I've used a felt inner sole inside the rubber boot. They keep your feet much warmer and dryer when standing on snow.

For those mountaineers who insist on wearing their Vibrams, it might be a good idea to buy some stretch rubbers to wear over the boots to protect the rawhide lacing.

CORDING SNOWSHOES - Snowshoes are essentially flatland devices, but more and more people are using them to climb slopes that wouldn't even have been attempted a few years ago. Some of my customers claim they have climbed ski slopes from bottom to top using corded frames and other gadgets.

Get two 8' lengths of 1/4" sisal rope or cord. Regular masking tape will keep the cut ends from fraying. Hold one end of rope along the bottom of one side of the snowshoe for 6", just inside the frame, up to the yoke, end pointing toward the heel. Wrap the remaining 7-1/2' around the rope and frame together, going through each space of the rawhide weave until you have made about seven turns. Then pull the remaining rope across to the other side and wrap it forward as before to the yoke, opposite the point at which you started. Tuck the end between the second set of turns and the inside of the frame, along the bottom of the snowshoe.

This cording has merit two ways. It improves the traction of the snowshoe, and it reduces the abrasion on the wraps of the rawhide around the frame, the points of greatest wear.

USED SNOWSHOES - After you have been out on a few trips, examine your snowshoes even if they are not broken. When they start looking worn on the bottom, here's a good trick. Brush boiled linseed oil all over the rawhide and wood and allow this to dry for at least 24 hours. This restores the color and resilience to the rawhide and wood. Add a couple coats of exterior grade spar varnish. Remember that rawhide is only a hard gelatin, and you really are walking on the varnish.

ABUSED SNOWSHOES - Then comes the fateful day when you check your snowshoes and see the rawhide lacing is worn and about to break or already broken. Don't panic; just follow these instructions. First, locate a piece of 1/4" width rawhide; some horse tackle shops carry it.

Cut the worn spot and trim back to good rawhide. Unweave about 6" of both ends, and balance the snowshoe so ends of raw-hide can be immersed in water for about 3". Soak ends for at least an hour, until rawhide is softened. Now, about 1/8" back from each end, make a 3/4" slit down the center of each strip. Next, take the extra strip of rawhide, which also has been soak-ing for the same length of time, and cut a similar slit in one end.

To attach, slide the slit in the extra strip over one end of the weave. Take the unslit end of the extra strip and push it through the exposed weave end slit. Pull on the extra strip until the slits are interlocked.

SNOW SHOE STRAP

Then take the unslit end of the extra strip and push it through the slit of the other end of the weave. Wrap the extra strip around the weave end to form a bight, and then push the extra strip end back through the slit in the opposite direction. It is now possible to pull on the bight to tension the rawhide, and then pull on the end projecting from the slit to lock the bight. Let the rawhide dry for at least 24 hours before oiling and varnishing, as recom-mended earlier. The suggestions included in this article, if followed carefully, should make your snowshoes last a long time.

> -- Excerpts from an article, "How to Maintain and
> Repair Your Rawhide Snowshoes,"
> by David Schonbrun

BUYING SNOWSHOES - Four factors should determine the type and size of snowshoe a person will choose to buy: 1) Maximum load to be carried by the snowshoe; 2) degree of maneuverability required by the snowshoe; 3) snow conditions; and 4) snowshoe quality.

EMERGENCY BOOTS - A friend once tried snowshoeing but didn't have hiking boots and couldn't find any to rent that day. So he wore plastic bags over his socks and tennis shoes over the bags. Said his feet stayed warm and dry. Enjoyed snowshoeing, too, in spite of the makeshift gear.

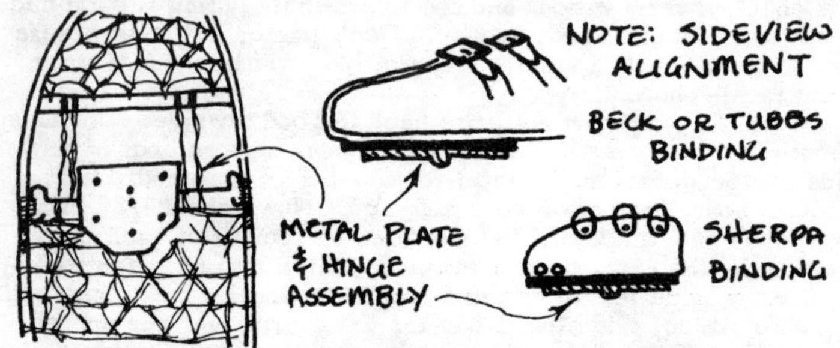

BETTER BINDINGS - Snowshoers are familiar with the problem of bad support in their bindings after turning tight hairpin turns while switchbacking or traversing steep slopes. The hinge-rod bindings stop most problems of this nature. A homemade version can be made using a piano-hinge design, costing very little in time or money.

Start with a pair of brass door hinges about 3-4" wide. Punch out the pin with a hammer and nail or saw the pin out using a hacksaw placed between the joints. Next, find a metal rod the same thickness as the pin and about a foot long. The rod should be made of softer metal than the pin but strong enough to support the weight of a snowshoer's foot.

Fashion a piece of lightweight metal into a shape like a truncated triangle as wide at the base as the hinge and longer than both halves of the hinge combined. Drill holes in the metal plate to match the holes in the hinge.

The best type of binding to use with hinge-rod arrangement is the Sherpa, but a Beck or Tubbs can be adapted. Position the metal plate on the bottom of the binding. The Sherpa binding should line up exactly even in front with the plate, but the Beck or Tubbs must line up where the binding folds up over the boot. Locate the holes on the binding and drill.

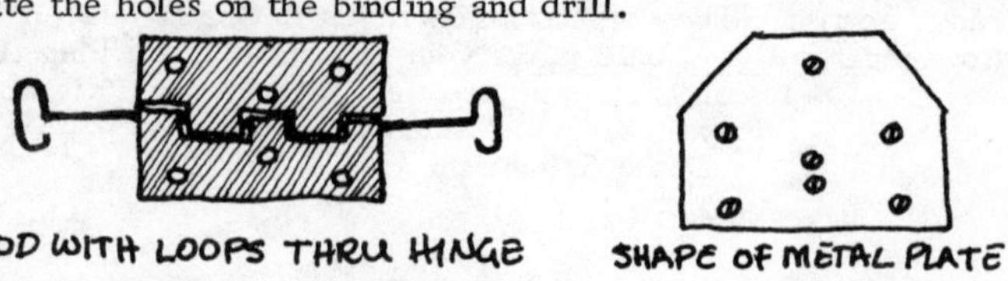

Assemble the parts together. The pin side of the hinge should be down and the plate goes between the hinge and the binding. Use brass bolts, washers and lock washers. Bend an elliptical loop about 1-1/2" long on one end of the metal rod using a vise and pliers. Push the rod through the hinge and then bend a corresponding loop at the other end. The overall length of the rod should be 2" shorter than the inside width of snowshoe frame.

Unlace the webbing in the area where the hinge-rod goes on the snowshoe. When relacing, thread the webbing through the loop and wrap it tightly around the frame. Each loop should be held by three pieces of webbing. (An alternative method is to attach the rod directly to the frame by drilling.)

Snow will stick to uncovered metal, so the parts must be covered with some type of wax, paint or a piece of vinyl tucked around the hinge and bolted into place. If the metal is not covered, snow will ball up around the binding causing problems in weight and balance. It may be necessary to lubricate the rod occasionally since the metal may deteriorate from wear and water. Use a thick bicycle or automotive lubricant.

-- Excerpts from an article, "Do-It-Yourself Snowshoe Bindings," by Richard E. Hanners

RUNAWAY STRAPS - Child's ski bindings don't have runaway straps included. You have to make your own, and the instructions are too sketchy for good results. Just tying a piece of nylon shoelace on is not enough. Even boxed sets of adult bindings don't always have runaway straps included. Sometimes they've been taken out of the package, and sometimes they've been forgotten. Always check on this when buying bindings. Length of strap and material of its construction are important and these matters shouldn't be left to chance.

But agreement is not total on whether or not it is desirable to have a runaway strap that will not break. Usually they're not supposed to, but could there be times when -- at least, under major stress -- the thing SHOULD break? A story was told to support the position that a runaway strap should NEVER break. Seems there was a girl skiing on Mount St. Helens who fell into a crevasse. Her skis hung up on the crevasse sides, and she hung there by her runaway straps until she could be rescued!

CHAIN REPAIR - Broken tire chains HAVE been repaired with carabiners. It's not the best idea in the world, but it could make the difference between staying there and getting out.

ROPE - If each member of a party would carry a 15' length of 1/4" nylon rope in his pack, it wouldn't be much of a burden for the individual. Yet, if any situations became dangerous or frightening, the lengths of rope could be easily tied together to provide a longer rope.

RENTALS - An idea for clubs which face equipment problems is
to establish a rental system. By renting, members can experiment with different types of equipment before buying. The club
also benefits by having a source of income.

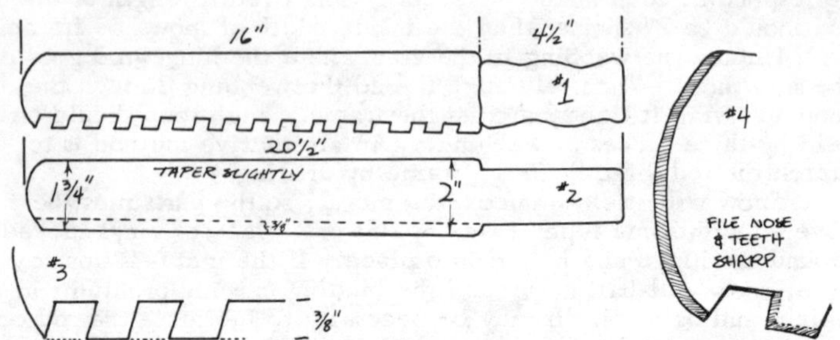

SNOW SAW - As lightweight winter camping and survival tools,
the snow saw and snow shovel are hard to beat. With them in
your pack you'll know you can survive the worst blizzard in the
quiet safety of a snow cave or igloo. Good aluminum shovels
are available to fit right onto your ice axe. For quickly cutting
blocks of snow, you need a snow saw. You can make one with
scrap and two hours' time that weighs as little as 5 ozs. Carry it
in your pack wrapped in a spare sock.

A finished snow saw should look like the drawing -- a jagged
strip of aluminum with a wood handle on one end. Here's what
you need: 1) A strip of stiff aluminum alloy about 21x2" from any
junk yard. Minimum thickness is 1/16"; use 1/8" for a sturdy job.
2) About a 6" square of 1/4" or 3/8" plywood. 3) Epoxy glue.
4) Tools, at least a hacksaw, file and pliers.

Cut the aluminum strip to the shape shown. Scratch a line
3/8" from the bottom as a base for the teeth, and mark out the
teeth. Cut slits down to the teeth base line with hacksaw and
wiggle holes off with pliers. Smooth out jagged bits with file.
File fronts and ends of teeth sharp, also tip of saw. Sandwich
blunt end between two pieces of glued plywood for handle; shape
to taste and varnish to seal out water.
                 -- Excerpts from an article, "Make A Snow Saw,"
                    by Tim Kendrick

(Ed. Note: Teeth are helpful but not usually necessary, according
to Off Belay's "Building Eskimo Snowhouses." The publication
states that since length of blade determines the size of snow block
that can be cut, 20" is the best length and 18" the minimum.
Also it suggests that handle and blade can be taped together and
then drilled for fastening with nuts and bolts.)

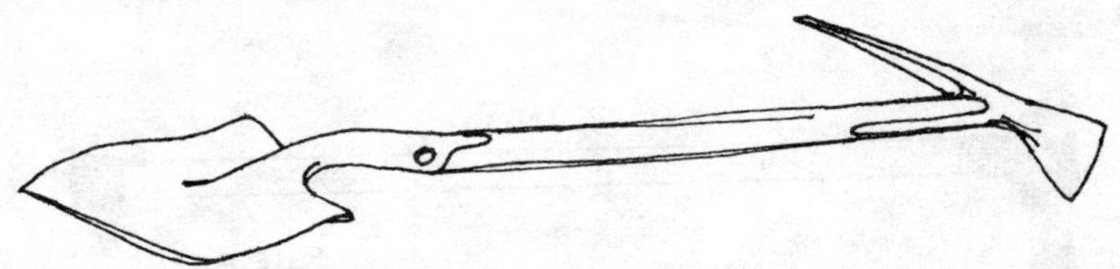

LAKE WENATCHEE TRAIL HELPER - This trail aid has been devised by District Ranger Richard H. Woodcock. He describes it
thus: Universally the most accepted walking stick is the ice axe,
and no hiker should be without one whether he expects to be
traveling steep snowfields or not. The ice axe has several uses
besides its primary one of chopping ice steps and effecting ar-
rests. However, its use can be greatly enhanced with an inexpensive and quick conversion. . .

A small camp shovel (made in Japan) is available for little
more than $1. All hikers should carry shovels, but few do. By
removing the shovel handle and slightly flattening the shank,
this shovel can be shaped so it will slip onto the tip of the ice
axe to the full length of the metal shank. A 5/32" hole drilled
through the ice axe shank, in line with the hole already in the
shovel shank, can be secured with a 5/32x1-3/8" aircraft bolt and
lock nut completing the half-hour conversion. . .

To keep the tool more handy as a walking stick, I use a
30 cm. Hope Alpinist ice axe and end up with an overall length
of 36-1/2". I then have a tool that will flick rocks and tree
limbs off the trail, bury excrement, put out fires, and so on. I
have dug many good-sized back country toilet pits with the Lake
Wenatchee Trail Helper and used it on several small fires. However, a person should be careful not to put undo strain on the
tool while digging. It is not as sturdy as a regular shovel. . .

When a person needs the ice axe for its primary use of ar-
rest, the shovel blade is easily removed. In my experience I
have found little need for removing the blade. And with the
additional uses engendered by the conversion, I wouldn't be
without it.

STAFF - Designed to do double duty as a walking aid and an
A-frame tent support is a bamboo staff one reader has developed.
The length of bamboo is cut off at the top just above one of the
joints and split lengthwise. At the top the two pieces are fastened together with a small hinge. At the bottom the pieces are
held together with a crutch tip. A means of holding the rest of
it together is still being worked out; both tape and string have
been tried and found unsatisfactory. The inside of the split bamboo staff is hollowed out to hold another stick, which is used as
the vertical rear support for the tent.

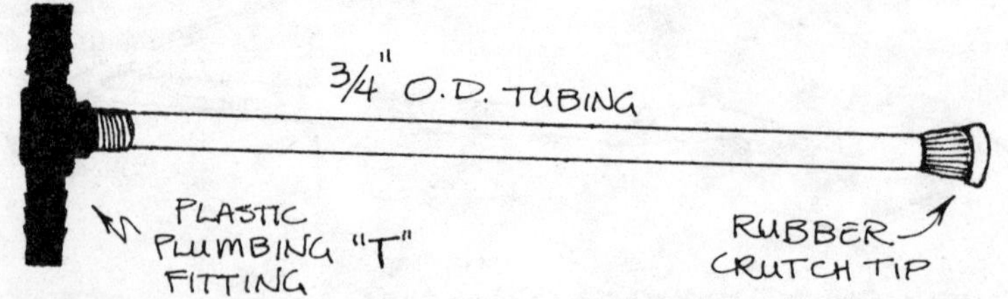

ALUMINUM WALKING STICK

WALKING STICK - Rock hopping across streams and other precarious places can be easier with a simple-to-make walking stick. Materials needed are a length of aluminum tubing, a rubber crutch tip, and a plastic "T" used in plumbing. The tubing generally comes in 6' lengths at most hardware stores. I used 3/4" O.D. tubing, cut into almost equal lengths (the shorter one was for my wife). I had to file away part of the plastic on the "T" to get it to fit inside the pipe for a handle, but the fit was snug and required no adhesives. Rubber crutch tips come in a variety of sizes, so make sure to get one to fit tightly over the other end of the tubing. Check the tip periodically to see that it hasn't worn through from abrasive use. Total weight is only a few ounces.

E-Z
THREAD
-R
4

ADVANTAGES - For all around good quality and styling combined with cost savings, the most rewarding way to get good sportswear is to sew it yourself. One can use either a kit or a pattern. Kits are perhaps the best way to start.

A kit is a wonderful bundle of ready-cut materials, thread, ribbons, grommets, zippers, pre-measured and pre-packaged down, pieces of Velcro, lacing, elastic, and good instructions. Briefly, it has absolutely everything you may think you will need plus a great deal more. A kit contains all the ingredients for completing a garment, tent, sleeping bag, mittens, those down booties that keep your feet so warm.

A kit will assure you a feeling of accomplishment, or fulfillment, when you sew your own sporting equipment. It will be something you do for yourself or for "yours." You worked on it; you put it together piece by piece as you checked off each step; and you saved money doing it! A poncho, for example, might cost $6 made from your own pattern, about $8 for a kit, and perhaps $18 for like quality readymade. A tent could run $40 homemade, $65 for the kit, and $150 for a comparable readymade. Down-filled booties might compare $7 to $10 to $15.

If you've never sewed anything before, cheer up! Almost everybody, sooner or later in their lives, has had some sort of friendly contact with a sewing machine. It doesn't really matter what kind either -- whether it's the big, highly advertised model or just little old Brand X.

One caution: If you are experienced, get hubby or the favorite boyfriend or even your older son to help. They can be excellent assistants, especially when it comes to following the kit or pattern instructions. The confident seamstress, with years of experience behind her, will attempt to do it her way at times and this is a very big "no-no!" Chaos can be the result. No matter how idiotic the instructions might seem to you, follow them religiously. Their writer has pioneered the kit the hard way and is passing on this learning to "lucky you!"

*

FABRICS - Once you've decided to take the big plunge, one of the principal things to consider is material. Garments, tents and packs designed for outdoor living are made of special materials unlike those of everyday clothes. You want to be certain that the material you select will serve its purpose. It is simply impossible to list here all of the materials that are available. There are just too many and there will be new ones tomorrow.

NYLON, however, is the reigning monarch of outdoor equipment -- there's no denying it. It is lightweight, strong and colorful. A bewildering array of choices is available, yet each is best suited for its own particular purpose. When sold it is specified by type and weight. Let's examine some of the basic types of nylon cloth, their uses and weights.

RIPSTOP NYLON is offered by the leading kit manufacturers in the 1.9-oz. category for jackets, vests, tents and sleeping

bags -- articles which need greater durability. The 1.9-oz.
means that one square yard weighs 1.9 ounces. Simple? Sure.

But what is ripstop nylon? Two heavy twisted threads are
woven into the fabric about 1/4" apart, thus forming 1/4"
squares. They usually can be seen by examining the material
while holding it up against good light. These squares make the
fabric extremely tear resistant, giving it its name "ripstop."
Incidentally, it is three times as tear resistant as fabric of like
weight but different composition. When choosing this material
or any article made of it, remember that as the weight decreases
so does the tear strength and abrasion resistance. These factors
cause reduced durability.

NYLON TAFFETA is a smooth-textured material frequently
used in ski jackets, down jackets and the like, where a fashion-
able, sleek, downproof, water repellent and wind resistant cloth
is desired. Nylon taffeta is specified not only by weight but also
by ply -- 2-ply is lighter than 3-ply. Ply refers to the number
of yarns twisted together to form a single thread. With its close
weave, it is not surprising that nylon taffeta is more abrasion-
resistant than ripstop nylon. But ripstop is the more tear resistant.

NYLON PACKCLOTH is the most tear and abrasion resistant, and naturally the most durable as well as heaviest. Resembling cotton duck, it comes in 7.5-oz. weight and is used mostly
for packs and similar heavy duty items. Don't worry if weights
vary a little, even as much as 10%, in nylon packcloth, since
manufacturing practices differ. Incidentally, while we're thinking of weights: The walls of a tent should never be lighter than
1.5-oz., and preferably 1.9-oz. fabric. Weaker material doesn't
have sufficient strength, and when a strong wind blows against
the tent the fabric can split, almost like an explosion.

POROSITY of material is an important factor in keeping
you comfortable in your garment. The weave of the fabric determines how much air passes in and out of the fabric -- how it
breathes. Nylon taffeta and ripstop are particularly effective in
keeping out the wind, yet permit body moisture to evaporate
outward. Let's suppose you bought a urethane coated (non-
breathing) jacket and sealed yourself into it. Very soon you
would be well on the way to getting wet from the inside out.
Your body moisture and radiated heat would not be able to escape and the result is a steam bath.

To check the porosity of any material, either hold it up to
a strong light to examine the closeness of the weave or, better
yet, try blowing through it and feel with your hand the amount
of air that passes through. Don't be ashamed to do it publicly
All you are doing is imitating the wind and, after all, it is your
money that you are planning to spend to get something which
suits your purposes.

Porosity is extremely important in down sleeping bags and
in tents. Every down bag must breathe to allow the down to
work properly. Don't panic if you see little pods of down float-
ing through the air, especially when you fluff a down bag or garment. You're not losing all the down, especially if it is a high
grade of down.

COATED NYLON, available under many brand names, is without porosity capabilities. This is a highly desirable feature for tent floors but not for jackets. Usually various types of nylon weaves, such as ripstop or taffeta of different weights, are coated with urethane. Blow as hard as you will, no air will pass through it provided it has been coated properly. This cloth is truly rainproof. It is not to be confused with water repellent cloth which is made of a closely woven material and will breathe.

SOME CHARACTERISTICS: NYLON is highly subject to heat; 482° F. will melt it. Those Delrin zippers have a melting point of only 330° F. A caution -- keep nylon away from the fire with its sparks and heat. Hope springs eternal, however, for you can mend those pesky little holes and snags with pressure sensitive ripstop nylon tape. Having done this, however, you no longer can have the article dry cleaned unless you don't mind replacing the tape after it comes back. Careful washing is all right. Never use bleach because it weakens nylon fibers.

Nylon edges ravel easily and so, in most kits, the instructions ask you to "heat seal" the edges. Literally translated that means melt the edges, usually with the aid of a candle. Scary? It sounds that way, but stay with it. Experiment with the little scrap pieces included in your kit for this and other purposes. Or test on some of the material you bought for sewing your pattern. Gently hold the very edge of the fabric to the middle of the candle flame. With a steady hand, no breeze and a little patience, you'll soon get over your apprehension and be able to seal yards of nylon in a reasonable time.

Nylon fabrics are prone to causing condensation although, unlike other materials, there is less water IN the fabric itself. Nylon feels wetter than other fabrics because the condensation stays on the surface and does not penetrate readily. For the same reason, nylon does not hold home-applied waterproofing very well.

COTTON, although it causes less condensation than nylon, does tear very easily. A greater tendency to mildew also could be a problem. If you're planning on applying a waterproofing compound to the object you are making, cotton would be a good choice. It absorbs the waterproofing agent better than nylon. Cotton also has come a long way since the introduction of synthetics. Now it is often blended with them -- for example, with nylon or dacron -- offering the best of both materials.

WOOL is the best companion in the outdoors. Warm, even when wet, it has helped many a hypothermia case from becoming a statistic in the obituary column. Although wool is relatively heavy, sometimes scratchy, easily abraded, and a prime meal for moths, don't go without it!

DACRON is a member of the polyester fiber family which is almost, but not quite, as strong as nylon. It also is not as elastic. Dacron is excellent when its thread is wrapped with cotton. ORLON, another synthetic, will not deteriorate upon exposure to sunlight as both nylon and dacron eventually will. Of course, unless you leave your tent set up year after year, this may not be a major consideration. Incidentally, orlon also has

the admirable quality of resembling wool after it is cut up and
spun into fibers.

*

INSULATION - Every sporting goods store worth its salt, or for
that matter any reputable catalog, will give you a detailed ex-
planation of sleeping bag or insulated jacket construction. But
here are a few points which may give you a little head start.
Internal construction refers to the manner in which a garment or
sleeping bag is filled with down, kapok, fiberfill or whatever.
You can't simply make a sack, stuff it full, sew it up and expect
it to serve the purpose. There are two major construction methods -- quilting and baffling.

QUILTING is done by placing two layers of cloth together,
filling, and then sewing through both layers. Most of us are familiar with this method -- great grandma and even grandma
made quilted blankets, often of brightly colored patchwork.
Although it is the least expensive, quickest and easiest method,
the results of quilting are cold spots because there is no insulation at the quilting seams. Therefore, such construction is not
advisable for cold weather clothing or sleeping bags.

In down-filled garments the greater the number of quilted
seams the less warm the garment will be. With quilting, the
down is too restricted, having little or, in extreme cases, non-
existent loft. Quilted jackets sometimes have a third, separate
layer of cloth attached to the inside or the outside which serves
as a wind break. For a warmer jacket, make sure it has that
third layer. Otherwise, whenever the wind blows you will have
to wear a windbreaker over it. I speak from experience.

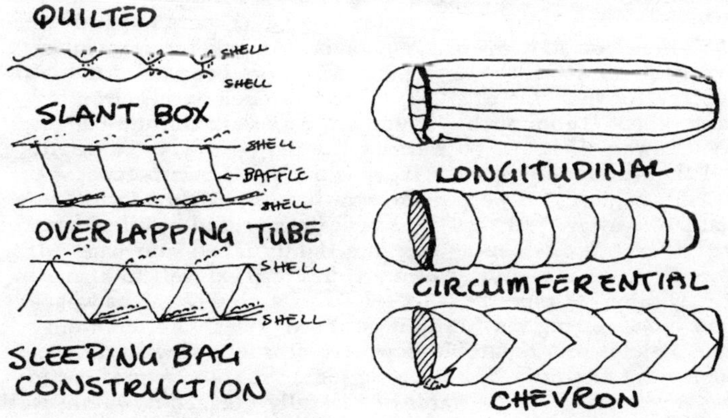

BAFFLING is a completely different technique wherein
pieces of thin cloth (usually a netting material) are sewed between the two main layers of cloth, forming separate compart-
ments which are then down-filled. Baffles prevent the filling
from moving about.

When the baffling technique is used for jacket construction,
we find a "longitudinal" design in even the better jackets. The

baffles are sewed from top to bottom which, upon closer exami-
nation, isn't much to write home about. The filling will eventually settle to the lower portions of the jacket, quite possibly
leaving you with cold shoulders. Sleeping bags with this type of
design have a tendency to act the same way.

The big word one sometimes sees in clothing descriptions,
"circumferential, " only means that these same baffles are sewed
from side to side. This does not permit the filling to shift down-
ward. Another method, not too common, called "chevron" has
baffles shaped like chevrons. Ready-made items must be
checked for baffle construction characteristics. Hold the article
up to the light to locate the seams and determine where the
filling has settled.

FILLING is the next important step. Let's be biased and
talk about the most expensive and best filler that I believe is
available today -- northern goose down. Down doesn't weigh
very much, keeps you warm and will last almost indefinitely if
you take proper care of it. Actually, it isn't the down that
keeps you warm; it's air! Trapped by these myriad down pods,
the air is heated by the body. It's this dead air space that
counts as insulation.

DOWN filling comes in two types, goose or duck. Which
one to use poses a good question. The geese and ducks that
provide down are usually raised commercially. Originally geese
were grown to a much larger size so the resultant down, a by-
product, was larger and less of it was required to fill things up.
But no more. The demand is now for smaller birds, so commercial goose down and duck down are about the same size.

Ounce for ounce, goose down is 10-12% more efficient than
an equivalent amount of duck down and 22% more expensive.
But before you start eyeing your favorite parakeet, remember
that duck down will be used more and more because of the high
demand for this type of filler. Goose or duck down? Don't
worry about it too much. If you are on a very limited budget,
duck down will keep you warm. The only way you can really
tell the difference between them is through a microscope.

If you get down wet, make sure it is thoroughly dry before
you put it away. Always store your down-filled article loosely.
Don't leave your sleeping bag in a tightly laced stuff bag. Also,
store it where it is dry. Down articles respond well to airing in
the sunshine. Drape them loosely over a clothesline or what-
have-you, letting the fresh air get at all sides. For cleaning,
take articles to a reputable down dry cleaner, or wash them at
home very carefully by following some suitable instructions to
the very letter. The rewards of carefully cleaned down are well
worth the trouble.

SYNTHETIC filling is available in several different kinds,
and it is a challenge to down. It is alleged to keep you warm,
dry rapidly and be lightweight. Polar Guard is one popular kind.
Another, Fiberbill II, was developed by the U. S. Army. It is a
filler with much promise. Kapok is well known, heavy and, of
course, utterly impossible if it gets wet. Even foam fillers are
used in some sleeping bags which, presumably, would be ade-

quate on a summer camping trip. Personally, I prefer my northern goose down mummy bag until convinced otherwise.

*

STITCHING - After all this about materials, construction and
fillings, there is still one more topic -- how to sew it all together. Previously I said almost anyone can sew from a kit or from a
pattern. With a kit the sewing is easier as the material is pre-
cut and all incidentals are provided. Also a kit includes fairly
simple instructions. Sewing from a pattern, though, isn't that
bad. Pick up a pattern, pick out an outdoor type material, and
begin. Some of the sporting goods stores, as well as the surplus
stores, carry the things you'll need. Don't get discouraged if
you don't find what you want right away, while shopping in the
local department stores or fabric and sewing centers. It's usually
available somewhere.

For example, have you ever wanted a good pair of rain
pants but shied away from the prices? Try getting a pajama pattern, or take an old pair to use as a pattern. Get the rainproof
material, the drawstring to hold them up, possibly a small zipper
for each pant leg (so you can slip the pants on without having to
remove your boots). Cut, and sew. Presto! A pair of rain
pants. Ponchos are popular in women's pattern books so pick one
up, buy the right fabric -- and don't forget to make the back
longer than the front so you can wear it over your pack.

When buying or making any garment for rain protection,
try to avoid having seams on the shoulders where water might
seep through. Good seam sealers are available for all outside
seams, but they must be reapplied from time to time.

Also make certain the outdoor garments you make will be
comfortable. Freely translated, that means loose clothing over
the outside, and inside clothing in layers for removal or addition
as the need arises. Also remember, tightly fitted raingear
causes overheating and condensation problems in a hurry.

In sewing remember that you don't want your article to
come apart at the seams as you're admiring the view from the
top of Mount Beautiful. Wear and tear on outdoor gear is far
greater than on a shirt or blouse for the office. You might want
to use different, stronger seams for outdoor clothing. In kits,
the manufacturer often recommends certain seams for certain
parts of a garment because, based on experience and experimen-
tation, he knows where the stress will be. Nylon taffeta and
ripstop have a tendency to stretch, especially if cut on a bias,
so don't pull them through the machine too vigorously.

ADJUSTMENTS will probably still have to be made before
taking that first stitch, because of the material. The needle you
are presently using may be too small. Get a larger size, possibly
a No. 20 but no smaller than a 16 or 14, depending upon how your
machine behaves. A ballpoint needle is preferable for synthetics
if your machine will take one, because it separates the fibers
rather than cutting through them. For all densely woven material
you'll need that larger needle so that there is a large enough hole
for the thread to slide through easily. If the needle is too small
the thread will ravel and break. This can cause a serious sewing

problem.   Test on a swatch of material first.   However, do use
the smallest needle you can; too large a needle leaves holes.

   If, after the use of a larger needle and lots of your patience,
your stitching still doesn't look right, then adjust the tension.   If
the loops of thread are even on the top and the bottom, the stitching is right.   If the top loop is bigger the top tension is too loose
and if the bottom loop is larger the top tension is too tight.   Adjust the tension accordingly, but do it slowly and very cautiously.
Your cost-cutting sewing machine might never make a perfect
stitch, so settle for the very best it has to offer.   (For instance,
coated tent material can be very, very trying.)

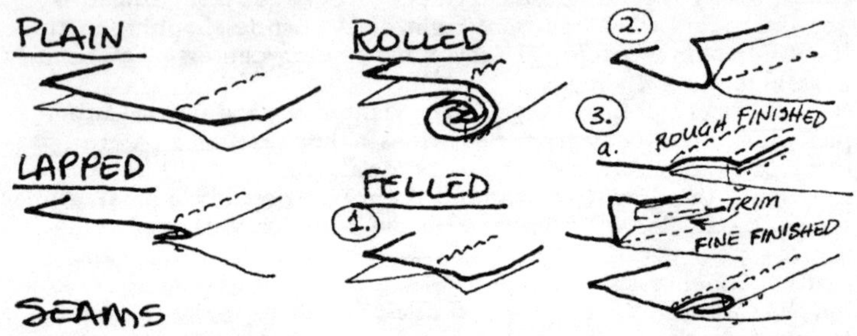

SEAMS

   SEAMS are a subject in themselves.   Let's start with the
felled seam, a super seam that holds it all together no matter
what happens.   It's no stranger; you've seen it on shirts.   To make
this seam put the fabric right sides together with the edges even
and stitch about 1/2" from the edge.   Then fold the 1/2" flap over
onto one of the fabric pieces and stitch it down along its raw edge.
For a finished felled seam, trim 1/4" off one of the 1/2" flaps and
fold the longer flap over the shorter. Then fold the whole thing
over once more in the same direction and stitch at its outer edge,
as before, to one of the fabric pieces.

   Then there is the rolled seam, which is sometimes used for
water repellent and waterproof materials or, for that matter, any
other fabric that will be exposed to "liquid sunshine" such as tent
flies.   In making this seam, the fabric is also placed right sides
together, edges even.   Now fold both edges off to one side by no
more than 1/4", then repeat the operation in the same direction
and the same amount. Finally, stitch through the center of the
resultant roll. What do you have when you finish all this rolling
and stitching? A very durable seam that is really quite simple
to make.

   The plain seam, of course, is the one in which you put two
pieces of material together with edges even and then sew a specified distance from the edge.   That's all really -- exactly what
the name indicates.

   Getting a little fancier, the lapped seam requires turning
the seam allowance of one piece of fabric under, laying the fold
over the seam allowance of the other piece (raw edges are together), and sewing the seam down through the overlap. Be sure
right sides of fabric are both up before sewing seam.

CONSTRUCTION comments that may also save problems: Let's say confusion rears its head. The solution is to baste when in doubt. That means to sew something temporarily into place, using big stitches which can be ripped out easily after the final sewing. It's even simpler to use sticky tape if you don't want to spend the time with needle and thread. Scotch tape is a little hard to peel off again, but masking tape and even that pink hair tape works very well. Special basting tape sold at fabric and notion shops works best. You can sew right along it and it rips off cleanly afterwards.

In selecting thread just use common sense. There is an almost infinite number of kinds and colors. A few inquiries will make clear the best thread for the job. All-cotton thread is being used less because the cotton-polyester works much better on today's synthetic materials. This is the kind of thread generally used for outdoor equipment. Nylon thread stretches and when used in sewing machines can be the source of a very frustrating time. Cotton-wrapped dacron has proved best in my experience.

Zippers are in common use today. When faced with putting in a zipper, a sewing machine zipper foot can be a very good investment. If you don't have one and don't want one, however, a zipper can be put in easily without one. They just aren't that hard. Just work slowly. Also, most commercial zipper packages have instructions printed either on or inside the package. The basic idea is: With right side of fabric and slide-tab side of zipper facing up, place edges of fabric over zipper to completely touch; baste zipper in place; separate zipper and stitch on right side of garment. Here again, tape can be used for holding the zipper in place. Special zipper-holding tape is available in most fabric stores.

Velcro is one of the modern age wonders. Made up of two pieces of material, one of hooks and the other of loops, it is the new way of holding things together. It's wonderful stuff, but sewing it is something else -- extremely slow going. The bottom tape is almost impenetrable with a needle because it is so tightly woven. Don't force your sewing machine; take it slow and easy. While you're at it, don't get the machine clogged with thread ends, down pods and other assorted lint. You'll be all day trying to pick it clean again. If necessary, tweezers work well for such an operation.

When sewing lightweight material, make sure you not only hold the material as it emerges from under the presser foot but hold the thread as well, at least until you have a pretty good start. This will prevent knotting the thread in a big mess on the under side of the seam you are sewing.

KITS need to be checked. Let's assume you've purchased a kit through the mail and the big day arrives. You've received it and are all ready to check it out. Do just that! Check it over very carefully against the parts list which is usually included. If there's something missing you'll have time to scribble a line to the company before you reach the point of being held up in your project. If anything is missing it may be one of the smaller items which is used toward the end. Don't forget that kits are put together by people just like you, who have been known to make mistakes. In addition, if you feel you're in trouble or something is drastically wrong with the instructions, don't hesitate to contact the company and ask about it.

-- Excerpts from an article, "Getting Started,"
by Rosemarie Rochlitzer

HEAVY DUTY SEWING MACHINE - Making your own camping products can be pretty tough on conventional sewing machines; industrial machines are very expensive, even used, considering the limited use they will receive from the hobbyist. A good substitute for an industrial machine is the old Singer sewing machine, such as the 1929 one that I have. These are converted from treadles by the use of a motor and work very well. They do not have a reverse.

Around 1950, Singer came out with a gear-driven machine which has a reverse. This is the one that I found would sew through 24 thicknesses of cotton cloth without difficulty. However, the one that I used would not accommodate as heavy a thread as I am able to use on the 1929 model. The 1929 model will sew No. 24 nylon or No. 20 cotton without difficulty, while the gear-driven model would not handle a thread heavier than No. 30.

Incidentally, use a straight needle if possible. A slant needle tends to distort thick seams.

WARM CLOTHES

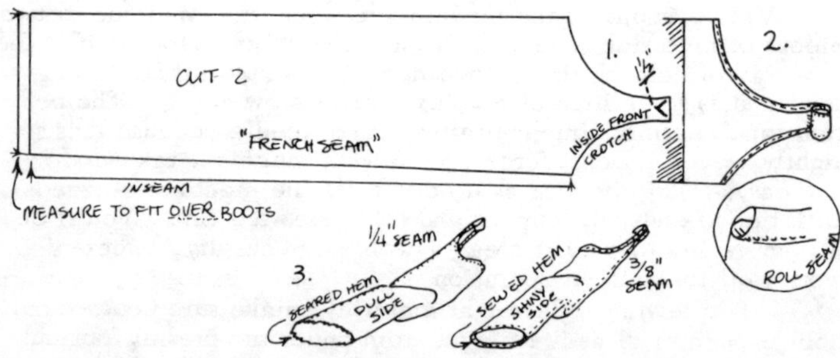

RAIN CHAPS - Why buy rain chaps when they can be made in less than an hour and for a fraction of the cost? Materials needed are: 1 yd. 45-55" coated nylon or other waterproof material; 2-1/2' grosgrain ribbon or cord; polyester thread; ballpoint needle size 14; very sharp scissors.

For a pattern, use old raingear cut apart, or lay the legs from a regular pants pattern together and guestimate the front and back crotch angles at the top (1) when cutting. Use sharp scissors, with a second person holding down the pattern so you won't have to prick the cloth with pins. Cut with pattern pieces

lying either lengthwise or crosswise of the fabric -- but not diag-
onally. Cut 2 crotch pieces 2" long to be used as reinforcing (2).

To sew, first roll hem along crotch angles (2), hemming in
the reinforcing piece at the same time. Remember, the shiny
side of the fabric is the waterproof side and should be placed on
the inside of the garment to prevent abrasion of waterproofing.
Stitch the grosgrain ribbon or cording to top, using a zigzag stitch
for strength, to make the ties. French seam the inseams (3).
Fold leg piece with shiny sides together and stitch 1/4" from
edges. Hold fabric securely while stitching -- it's slippery. Do
not pin, or pin only in seam allowance. Turn leg inside out so
seam is on the inside (shiny side is now out). Stitch seam again,
3/8" in. This seam is good because it is strong and durable,
gives the inside of the garment a finished appearance, and only
produces one set of stitching holes to waterproof. Either roll-hem
leg bottoms or sear with soldering iron (carefully!). Some people
recommend hemming legs for strength. Others say not to --
hems collect mud and water.

Waterproof all seams with seam sealer. Chaps are now
finished!

RAIN PANTS - If one wishes to make rain pants, an easy method
is to use a pajama pattern. If you already own pajama bottoms
made out of the pattern, try them on over your hiking clothes
for size. I used 1/8" shock cord for the waist and cuff closures
as they can be left open for ventilation or tied, and you will still
be able to remove the pants without untying them which can be
difficult with cold wet hands.

DOWN VEST - The vest is a practical garment -- lightweight,
comfortable and nonrestrictive -- and it adapts well to the "layering" system. A vest that will serve many years can be made
in an afternoon. You'll need, of course, a sewing machine; we
suggest a ballpoint needle and cotton covered polyester thread.

Separating zippers are available at local fabric stores, lug-
gage or sleeping bag manufacturers, or outdoor equipment retail-
ers. Nylon ones usually work easier than the metal and they
won't freeze up in cold rainy weather. A two-way zipper which
has two pulls and can be zipped up from the bottom allows un-
hindered leg movement, especially important if you plan to sew
a longer-than-waist length vest.

Zipper length varies with the size and style of vest. For the
turtleneck design shown here, in which the zipper extends to the
top of the collar, about a 24" zipper is required for a men's size
medium, or 26" for a size large. (Most commercially made
down vests are constructed so that the zipper does not extend onto
the collar.) Sewing cord or string into the edge of the zipper
flaps keeps the material from catching in the zipper pull. You'll
need about 8' of cord.

Ripstop nylon is a good fabric choice for this garment. It's
strong, durable, lightweight and crushes easily into small pack-

ing spaces. About 2-3/4 yards of 45" fabric are required for a men's size medium vest.

Vests are usually stitched through (quilted) in three horizontal lines to keep the down filler from shifting. It is possible to construct a down vest with baffles if you wish. Baffling separates the lining from the outer shell of the vest, allowing the down more lofting space. The result is a warmer garment.

We don't recommend baffling a vest, however. Lynn once made a down sweater with baffles, which proved to be a rediculous waste of valuable time. Aside from making her feel and look like a stuffed armadillo, the baffling afforded her plenty of room so she filled the sweater with too much down (a common beginner's mistake), making it too clumsy and too warm to be comfortable. She also learned that in many ways a down vest is preferable to a down sweater or jacket. The vest is more versatile (allowing layering), more comfortable (not so bulky), easier to make (no sleeves), and cheaper (less materials needed).

Despite our advice, if you do decide to baffle a down vest or sweater, sheer or regular nylon tricot is an easily available material to use for baffling. Most fabric stores carry it in their lingerie fabric section.

The final important material to consider is the down. A men's medium vest takes about 4 ozs. of down.

CUTTING - The most important thing to remember when cutting out your vest is to cut it much larger than you think you will need it. Probably when your vest is completed you'll wish you had made it larger still.

Use any pattern -- a commercial one or make your own from a comfortable shirt or jacket or even pajama top. Draw around your garment, then enlarge that pattern by 2-3" all around. If you have an eye for size, the finished pattern should look much larger than the finished vest will be. Cut the lining slightly smaller than the outer shell; you need to allow the down room to loft. A half-inch differential is good.

For this turtleneck style, you need to cut only one rectangular collar piece. Cut it large -- you can always trim it later. Some down vests are made with a ribbed nylon or cotton collar instead of a down-filled one. You may prefer this. Ribbing is available by the yard in all colors at fabric stores. Again, variations in the construction of the vest may be necessary in order to attach a different type of collar.

CONSTRUCTION - Sew shoulder and side seams of both lining and outer shell. All seams should be about 1/2". Sew one edge of collar piece to outside shell neck edge (1).

Cut two pieces of cord or string the length of the vest front including collar. On both front edges of outer shell, fold fabric under 5/8", folding over the cord, and stitch cord tightly into fold (2). A zipper foot is helpful here. Sew zipper to lining front (3) turning lining edge in 3/4" and top-stitching on wrong side of zipper tape. The top of the zipper should extend 2-1/4" beyond neck edge.

Pin lining against outer shell making neck edges even. Turn

DOWN VEST

31"
10"
8"
8"
9½"
OUTER VEST BACK
CUT 2
lining ½" smaller
20"
OUTER VEST FRONT
CUT 2
lining ½" smaller
28"
27"
POCKET (OPTIONAL) CUT 2
10"
9"
6"
5"
COLLAR CUT 1
20"
(1)
NECK EDGE
COLLAR
(2)
COLLAR
OUTER FRONT
CORDING OR STRING SEWN IN
(3)
LINING FRONT
WRONG SIDE OF ZIPPER
2¼"
(4)
FINISHED ARMHOLES
COLLAR
TOP OF ZIPPER
2. TURN COLLAR DOWN INSIDE
1. PIN LINING WITH ZIPPER ON INSIDE
OUTER FRONT
3. STITCH ¼" FROM CORDING STITCH
(5)
LAST LINE
STITCH THIS LINE FIRST
SECOND
6"TO 6½"
(6)
VELCRO CLOSURE (INSIDE)

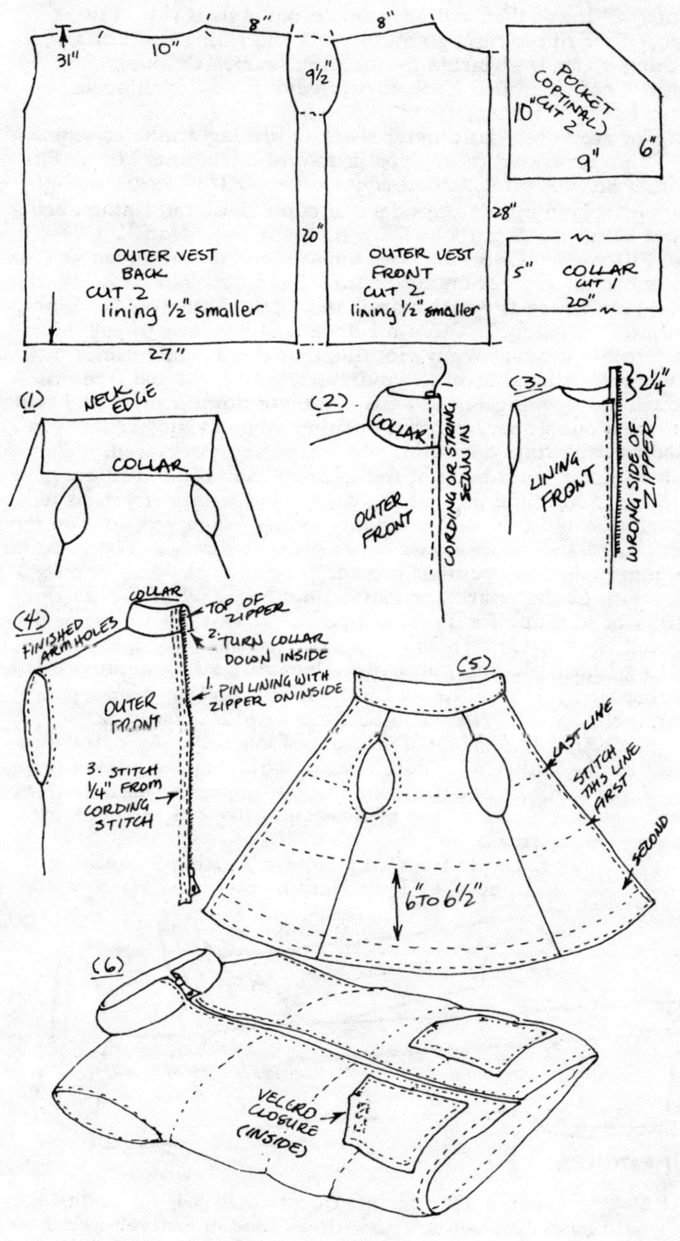

in front edges of collar. Turn collar down to lining on inside to
about 1/4" lower than collar seam on outer shell (4). Pin in
place. Sew zipper through outer shell and lining and collar,
stitching about 1/4" inside the cording seam. On outer shell,
topstitch collar around neck edge, leaving a 5" opening in the
center back for filling.

For armholes, hold outer shell and lining armholes together. Clip curves and turn edges in toward each other 1/2". Pin
together and topstitch folded edges together 1/8" from edge of
armhole. Turn up bottom edges of outer shell and lining about
1" and hem, leaving about 7" in the back open for filling.

Fill vest. If working with unpackaged down, move as if in
slow motion. Do not create breezes by fast movements. Work
someplace where it won't matter if a little down gets on things,
like inside a garage. Close all doors and windows to get rid of
any possible drafts. Wear clothing that down won't stick to.
Slowly take a handful of down and put your hand and forearm
through the opening in the vest. Release down inside, and bring
your hand out slowly, closing opening around your hand as you
withdraw it. Stuff the collar piece first and pin closed. Then
work with the main body of the garment. Pin it closed every
once in a while and pat out the down to ascertain if you have
enough (the old trial and error method!). When you do, pin the
hem closed and shake excess down off vest slowly. Then stitch
the hem and neck openings closed.

With chalk, mark horizontal lines every 6" or 6-1/2" from
bottom of vest up, for quilting lines. Pat vest until down is dis-
tributed equally throughout, and pin outer shell to lining along
quilting lines, placing pins every 4" or so. Stitch center quilting line first (5), then lower line. Stitch top line from zipper
to armhole on each front and between armholes on back.

If desired, sew pockets to front of vest (6). An extra flair
would be the addition of Velcro stripping along the pocket openings to prevent loss of articles when vest is packed upside down.
Also, you might add a loop at the center back of the neck for
hanging and storing.

-- Excerpts from an article, "Getting Something
Done," by Lynn Harding and Julie Winn

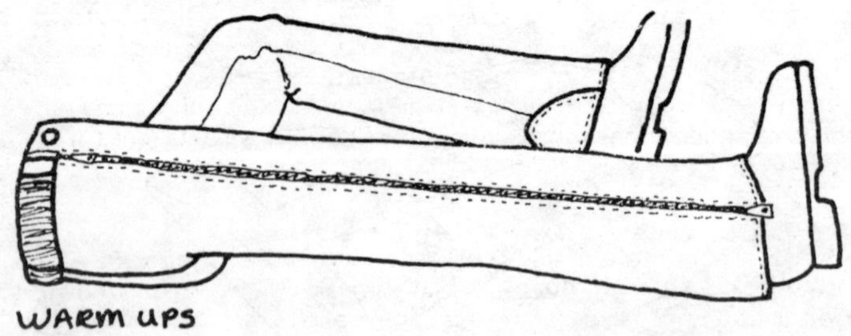

WARM-UP PANTS - This garment cost about $20 for materials
but would have cost perhaps four times that in a store. (All materials were purchased, along with considerable advice and

counsel, from a local home economics teacher, proprietor of a service to would-be outdoor sew-it-yourselfers.) The exterior layer is K-Kote nylon, the inside layer is Fiberfill II quilted to nylon. Inside each pant leg is a built-in gaiter with Velcro fastenings which snugs around the boot top to keep out powder snow.

These materials are very slippery and hard to work with, definitely not a sewing task for beginners. I washed the Fiberfill before cutting out the pieces, following good advice that the quilting is done with thread which may shrink, although the Fiberfill II and the nylon fabric will not. The two 40" zippers also were pre-shrunk to be certain the cotton fabric which supports the nylon teeth would not change size after the garment was completed. All the elastic used in the garment also was pre-shrunk just to be sure.

Side seams were left open 6-8" and top front was faced with a 1" hem. Back had waistband elastic stitched into a 1" turndown. Then about a 3" strip of Velcro was stitched to each side at the top for quick and easy loosening for removal. With side seams open, the wearer can easily reach into pants pockets, underneath.

The zippers have sliders at each end, for easy on-off and increased ventilation, if needed. The seams were waterproofed on the inside with a small amount of sealant which came with the other materials. It did not discolor the fabric and the odor was much less persistent than Pliobond.

The half-circle bootguards on the inner edge of the pant bottoms were made of real leather. The vinyl or imitation I have seen on some store-bought warm-ups is reputed to wear out very quickly. I bought leather elbow patches at the notions counter for these protective appliques.

This garment was made using the Daisy Kingdom master pattern, Warm Up Pants #5, which can be used for extra small through extra large sizes.
-- Excerpts from an article, "Warm-Up Pants for
Twenty Bucks," by Ruth Munson

SLACKS - People who have difficulty finding ready-made slacks suitable for hiking but are handy at sewing may be happier making their own. An old pair of slacks that has proven comfortable may be used as a pattern. Make big pockets; perhaps one could be waterproof for collecting damp objects like beach agates. Wool is expensive per yard, but it is wide and a little goes a long way.

GAITERS - Materials needed: 3/4 to 1 yd. 45" waterproof nylon packcloth; 2 - 15" separating nylon zippers; 10 snaps; 8 grommets; 1-1/2 yds. 5/8" elastic; nylon flat lacing 3/8" wide (enough to go through the calf casing of each gaiter, about 64"); 4' cording; 2 boot hooks; leather reinforcement pieces; polyester thread.

Cutting: Make a pattern according to the drawings (Fig. 1)

using newspaper, tissue paper or (for longer life) thin Pellon.
Lay pattern pieces out on folded cloth and cut.

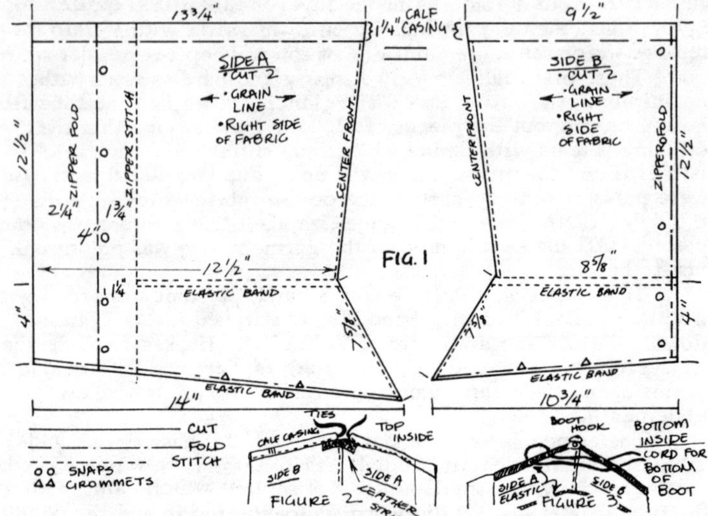

Sewing: Coated side of fabric is inside of gaiter. Join center front seams, using flat-felled seam; stitch to just below top casing fold line, 1-1/2" from top of gaiter. Fold calf casing under and stitch down, leaving ends open at center front where nylon drawstrings will come out. Using a 5/8" square of leather, reinforce where front center seam ends and casing begins. Stitch across and around leather square several times (Fig. 2). Run a 16" piece of the nylon lacing through each side of the calf casing; stitch one end of one lace down at the zipper stitching line on side A and one end of the other at zipper fold line on side B (Fig. 2)

Turn lower edge under 3/8" and sew elastic along turned edge, stitching twice, about 1/8" in from each side of elastic. Elastic should run from zipper stitching line on side A to zipper fold line on side B and be reinforced by stitching several times at each end.

Attach ankle elastic from zipper stitching line on A to zipper fold line on B, sewing twice, 1/8" from each edge.

Attach four grommets through elastic and fabric at bottom edge of each gaiter, reinforcing the grommets with 1" square pieces of leather (Fig. 3). Lace cording through grommets to fit under boot instep. Tie cording ends together on outside of side B. Attach boot hook to each gaiter at center front point, using a small piece of leather as reinforcement.

Turn under on zipper fold line on side A to form overlap and attach snaps to inside of overlap, 1-1/4" from zipper stitch line. Space snaps so that two are below ankle elastic and three above. Sew other half of snaps 1" in from fold line on side B.

Attach zippers. Fold top of each side of zipper tape down 1/2", and place on gaiter so teeth begin about 1/2" below the top. Place one side of zipper on inside of side A overlap, along zipper stitch line. Stitch down double for strength. Turn back 3/8" at side B zipper fold line and attach other side of zipper as above. On both sides of zipper stitch extra at tops and bottoms of tape for reinforcement.

-- Excerpts from "How to Make Gaiters," Signpost
Bulletin No. 3

SLEEP OUTFITS

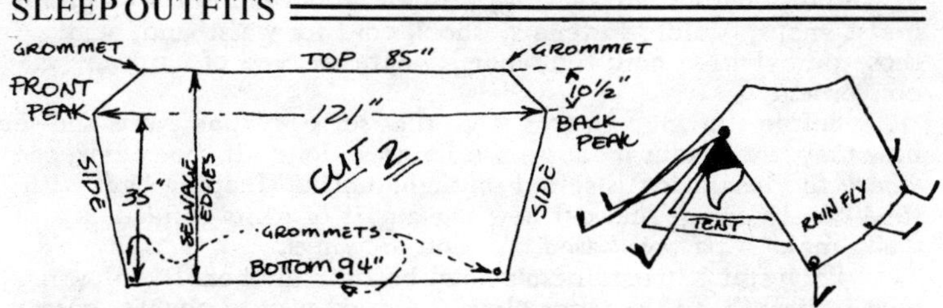

RAIN FLY – Solve the water repellency and condensation problems in your tent by making a lightweight rain fly. It's easy and saves you $$. These directions are for a 5x7' tent with A-shape pole arrangement in front or one center pole in front and one in back. Two grommets in the fly, above the poles, hold the fly taut lengthwise, and grommets or loops on the sides hold it out away from the tent so water will run off at some distance from the tent.

Materials needed are: 7 yds. 38–45" water repellent or coated nylon fabric, lightest weight; 8 – 1/2" grommets and a way of putting them on, or enough 1/2" or 3/4" webbing for 8 loops (about 4') and 2 grommets; some plastic or leather pieces for reinforcement where loops are attached; 24 ft. or so of light-weight strong cord; 6 or 8 tent stakes, depending on whether or not you need a middle stake on each side; thread.

Cut fabric to dimensions shown here and mark position of top grommets (85" apart) with a pen or permanent marker. After cutting one end lay it against the other three to get four the same. Sew two pieces together across top between grommet positions and down to peaks at each end, using a flat-felled seam. Hem ends and sides, using a rolled hem. Be careful not to stretch the fabric unnecessarily when hemming. Cut the reinforcement pieces and sew to top seam grommet positions, the 2 end peaks, 4 corners, and the middle of each side. Attach the grommets and loops. Run cord through all except two top grommets and cut to desired length.

BIVOUAC PANTS - Most insulated pants are filled with down. With the advent of continuous filament polyester fill, several key disadvantages of down can be circumvented. Polyester fill is cheaper, warmer when wet and very easy to work with. But, not to be biased, it is less loftable and a little heavier. Yet, if

the weather is inclined to be wet, it comes out on top. And since
it is easy to work with, anyone can make bivouac pants at home.

The following materials are needed: 1) Zippers -- Talon
coil works best. Measure for length along inseam of a pant leg
from ankle to groin. Be sure they match up and are the separating type. 2) Fabric -- about 6 yds. 45" wide. Ripstop is strong
and light but lets in wind and water. A super combination is
60/40 in front and taffeta in back, although this is heavier. The
front fabric at least must be breathable to compensate for condensation due to body heat. 3) Polyester fill -- various kinds are
available; check them out. 4) Miscellaneous hardware -- grommets, snaps, Velcro fasteners, shock cord for waistband, and
those push-button cord tighteners, whatever type of hardware is
convenient.

Before starting, go to a store that sells bivouac pants and see
how they are made; measure the lengths along all the seams; see
where the insulation is sewed through, unlike sleeping bags with
tube construction; find out how big a pair of pants is needed.
Then make a pattern based on some drawings.

Polyester batting doesn't need baffle chambers like down.
Sew it directly to the outer cloth. A good way to counter cold
spots along the seams is to overlap layers of batting from the
outside pants fabric to the inside pants fabric. But don't make
the insulation layer more than 1-1/2" thick. The outer pants are
slightly larger than the inner pants (differential cutting), giving
room for the batting to expand. The inner pants should be cut
to your real measurements.

Attach the zippers along the inseam, one on each leg. Be
sure they are reversed so you can unzip the individual legs, separate the zippers, and then join the legs to make a bivvy, or
half, bag. Finish by turning outer pants over inner at the waist
and sewing in a hollow hem, or casing. Insert shockcord as a
waistband, or use nylon cord and tighteners, Velcro, etc.
-- Excerpts from an article, "Polyester Insulated
Bivouac Pants, " by Richard Hanners

DOWN SLEEPING BAG - "I just can't use this bag any more! I've
got to get a new one! . .Hey, I know! I'll make my own! . .
Of course, I'll need a few things like 10 yds. of downproof ripstop nylon or taffeta, about 55 yds. of tricot nylon net, dacron
thread, and down (or Dacron II, if I can't salvage enough down
from my old bag). "

Early next morning, Joyce ripped open her old bag, sewed
the down into pillowcases, cut two 90x45" and two 90x36" taffeta strips and marked each with chalk lines 9" apart, leaving a
4-1/2" margin at top and bottom on the 90x36" sheets. These
measurements make a rectangular bag. Joyce, wanting to make
a mummy bag, cut a cardboard triangle as a pattern for shaping
the bottom sides.

Using the largest stitch and loosest tension on her home sewing machine, Joyce sewed the two larger sheets together on one

DOWN SLEEPING BAG

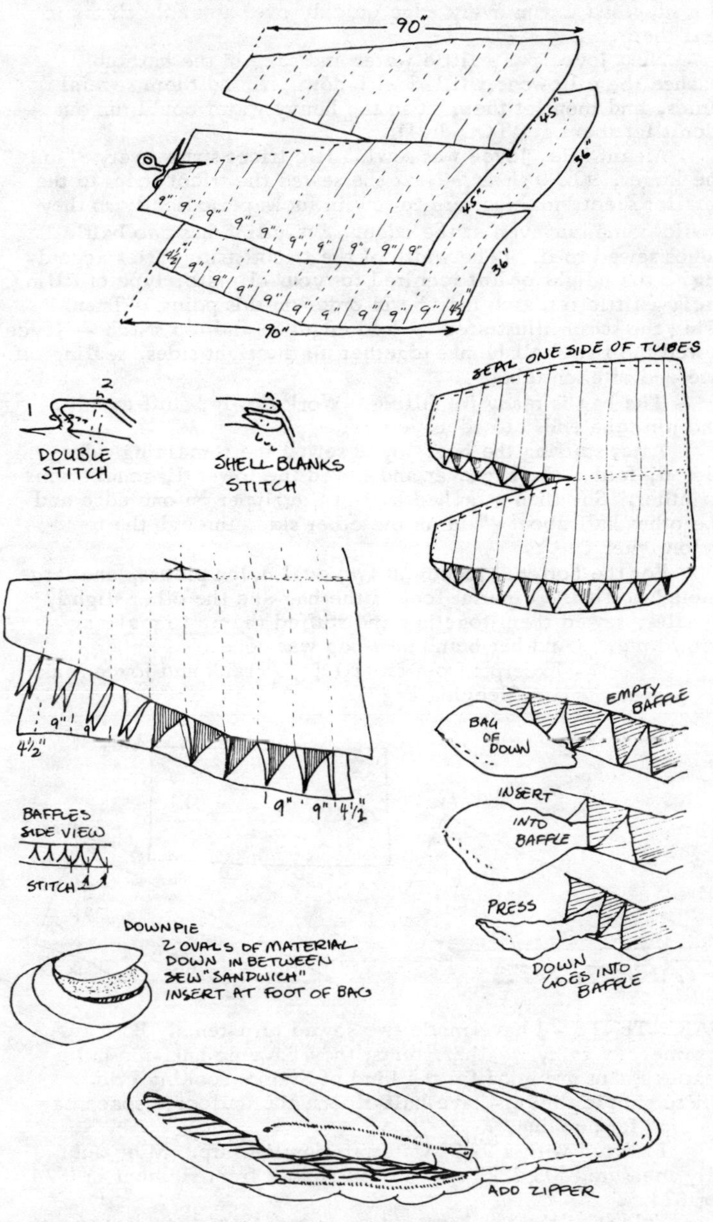

side using a flat felled seam, then the two smaller sheets. "Now I'm supposed to run every edge quickly over a candle flame to seal them. "

Next Joyce put a little water and soap in the bathtub, washed the pillowcases filled with down, rinsed them several times, and then let them sit so the heavy water could run out (don't let them get TOO dry!).

Meanwhile, Joyce was sewing two tricot strips every 9" on the larger, 90x90 sheet. Next she sewed the tricot strips to the smaller sheet, making sure to sew in tucks periodically so they would come out even at the edge. Every line has two baffle edges sewed to it. (The width of the tricot strips varies according to the height of loft required for your climate, type of filling, etc.; a little research may be in order on this point.) Then, using the stitch illustrated -- fold edges in and top stitch -- Joyce sewed the two shell blanks together up the right sides, sealing off one end of each tube.

The bag is ready for filling. Work slowly, stuff evenly, and pin tube ends closed as you go.

After stuffing the bag, Joyce sewed the remaining sides closed, folded the bag over and sewed the lower diagonal seams together. She then attached half of the zipper on one edge and the other half about 4" in on the other side, through the top nylon layer ONLY.

For the bottom, Joyce cut two oval nylon pieces, one large enough to fit the circular foot of the bag and the other slightly smaller, sewed them together and stuffed them, to make a "down pie." And her brand new bag was done!
<blockquote>-- Excerpts from an article, "Frank and Joyce Make A Sleeping Bag"</blockquote>

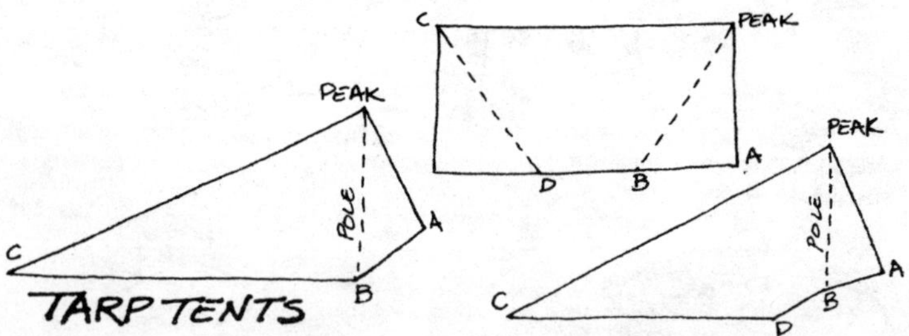

TARP-TENTS - I have made two sewed tarp-tents. Both are summer, or rainy weather, tents; they have no anti-mosquito features, but are good for the kind of Sterno-cooking I do. These simple shelters have half-floors; the unfloored space can be used for cooking.

I started with a 9x10' waterproof nylon tarp. Mine actually measured 105x122" and was purchased from Holubar in 1974 for $23.

Fold it so the two short sides are together, then sew one of what is now the sides together. The other short side is sewed

together for a foot or two from the fold and will be the doorway.
When set up, the interior dimensions will be about 7x7'. The
entrance will require two sectional poles, each about 6' long,
which fit up into the peak and provide an A-shaped cross section. I marked my pole sets: A-1, A-2, A-3, A-4 and B-1, etc.

The second tarp-tent I made was from a 10x10' tarp because I couldn't find a 9x10' (L.L. Bean, $24.50). Fold in half
and sew BOTH short ends. This makes an interior about 7x8',
with a door 3' high and a peak height of up to 8'. You will
need two poles 7' or 8' long, or one center pole 6-1/2' or higher
(great for a tall person).

All measurements are approximate, because you can mod-
ify them by the angle at which you pitch the tent and the length
of pole you use.

LIGHT TENT - To make a tent similar to the Stephenson Warmlite, cut one king-size and one regular-size bed sheet (preferably
percale) into four pieces for the floor, back, top and front.
Waterproof and dye sheets with a liquid waterproofer and paint
pigment in your bathtub. Lace sheets to curved plastic pipe.
Needs four stakes. Weighs 7 lbs. "I made mine eight years ago
and it's still perfectly serviceable."

BACKPACKS

CHILD CARRIER - This wrap-around carrier is comfortable for
the mother, secure for the child, and creates a closeness most
commercial carriers cannot provide. It can be tucked into a very
small space when the child is walking. All it requires is a piece
of strong cotton -- washed denim is best -- about 10" wide and
12-1/2 feet long.

To put it on, the mother squats and the child stands behind
her, against her back, as if for a piggyback ride. Midpoint of
cloth is wrapped around baby's back, pulling ends under baby's
arms and over mother's shoulders. Ends are then crossed over
mother's chest and under her arms to the back again. Here the
fabric crosses again, covering and supporting child's hips, and is
pulled forward from there at mother's waistline and tied securely
in front.

RUCKSACK - Here is the world's first rucksack made from one
piece of cloth, one piece of webbing and one button (plus a little
Velcro and a scrap or two of cloth). The weight is supported by
the webbing "frame," preventing the nylon fabric from stretching as it might if straps were simply sewed on top and bottom.

Materials: 1 yd. coated nylon packcloth, at least 40" wide;
14' of 1" nylon tubular webbing; 10" of 1" Velcro tape; 1 large
button (carve your own from a piece of hardwood); thread, cotton

covered polyester suggested because it is much stronger than plain cotton and works well in most sewing machines. Total cost of materials, about $7.

First familiarize yourself with the design. Read all instructions completely before beginning. Next, lay out the nylon cloth with coated or shiny side down. Smooth out wrinkles with an iron on low setting. Draw pattern on cloth, using a soft lead pencil or tailor's chalk. A large carpenter's square comes in handy for keeping things properly aligned. Then cut around the outer edge of the drawing; do not cut any of the inner lines. Use (1) for pattern and (2) for general orientation throughout.

Hem the edges of the back panel and the top edge of the top panel. When doing the sides of the back panel, sew only down to the edge of the back panel; do not continue on to the bottom panel. Using the dotted lines on your pattern as a guide, fold the weather seal sections as shown and pin them in place (3). Be careful in arranging the lower end of the seal and particularly be sure that the diagonal made by the fold crosses the corner of the side panel. The doubled edge will be the weather seal of the pack and the arrangement at the lower end of the edge is so that the back panel can be folded into the slot between the double edges when the pack is assembled. Sew along the lines that mark the edges of the side panels, being careful that you catch the folds in the stitching.

Now for the webbing. Cut a 10" piece from the 14' length and singe both ends of both pieces to keep them from raveling. Set the 10" piece aside. Place the center of the long piece in center of bottom edge of front panel, and pin it in place. Sew webbing in place along bottom edge, stitching to about 2" from corners of front panel, at least two lines of stitching along the webbing. Make corner loops, using about 8" of the webbing (4); then pin webbing along sides of front panel and sew into place, again stopping about 2" from corners. With the 10" piece of webbing, make a loop and sew it into place along the top edge of front panel (5). Anchor the loops with plenty of stitching at each of the corners. The upper corners have three layers of webbing; I had to use a hand awl on mine.

Next is the button tab (6). From one of your scraps cut a 2x7" piece of nylon and sew it as shown. Pin on underside of top panel so triangular part of tab sticks out past edge of panel and sew in place. Be sure slot in tab is large enough for your button.

The rucksack is assembled inside out. The bottom and back panel fold upward, with the back panel fitting into the slot of the weather seal. The top panel folds down and is sewed to the upper edges of the side panels. Be careful at the corners that the edges of the side panels match the edges of the bottom and top panels. This is awkward because the webbing makes everything lumpy. Use lots of pins. Turn the pack rightside out, place the back flap in the slots of the weather seals, and pin it into place. Sew about 5" up the sides. (To get the pack into the sewing machine, I found it necessary to turn it inside out again.) Anchor upper ends of weather seal flaps in top panel and sew button on back flap.

RUCKSACK

(1)
2"
5"
5"
TOP PANEL
1½"
WEATHER SEAL
SIDE PANEL
4½"
2"
FRONT PANEL
15"
5"
3"
18"
BOTTOM PANEL
1"
5"
15"
HEM EDGE 1"
BACK PANEL
11"
5"
(2)
WEATHER SEALS
TOP
SIDE PANEL
FRONT PANEL
BACK PANEL
BOTTOM PANEL
FOLDED VIEW
(3)
CORNER OF SIDE PANEL
STITCHING
WEATHER SEAL (COATED SIDE) DOWN
(4)
(5)
(6)
MAKE TUBE COATED SIDE OUT
TURN TUBE INSIDE OUT
RUN A FEW LINES OF STITCHING
FOLD & STITCH

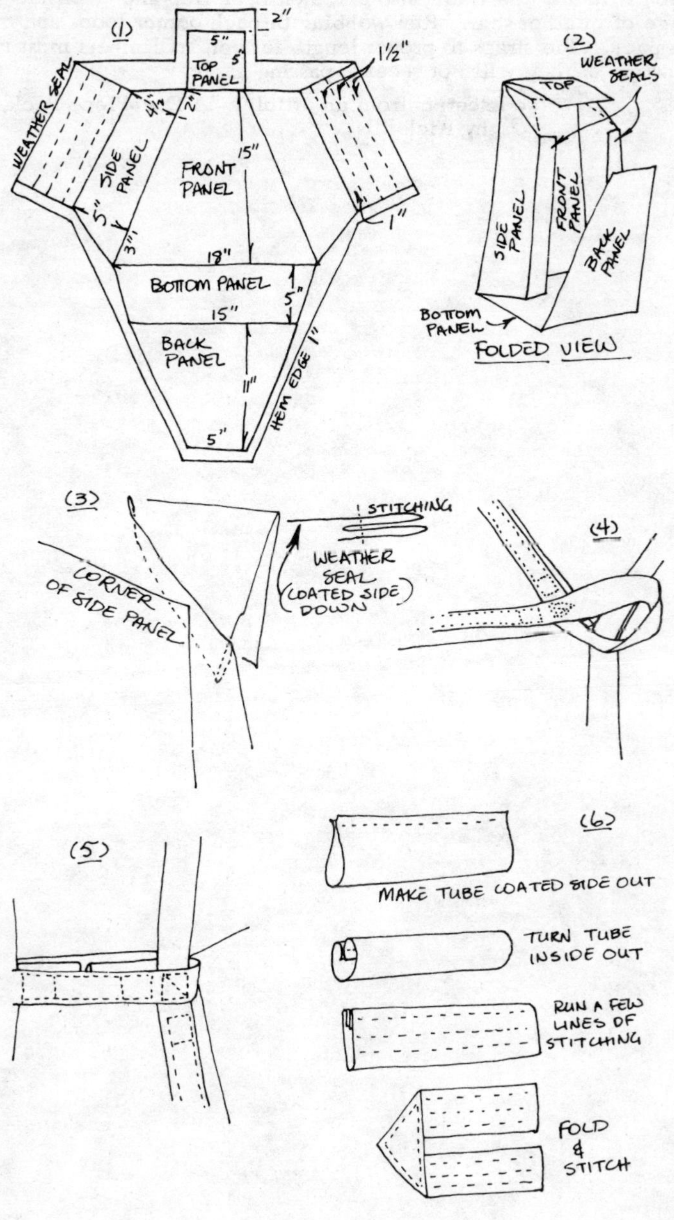

Cut Velcro into two 5" pieces, separate the two sides of
each strip and sew them into place on back flap and on inside
edge of weather seal. Run webbing through corner loops and try
on pack. Tie straps to proper length for you. Climbers must use
bowline or they will not receive passing grade.

    -- Excerpts from an article, "A One-Piece Pack, "
      by Rick Ells

CHAPTER 5
Special Interest Stuff

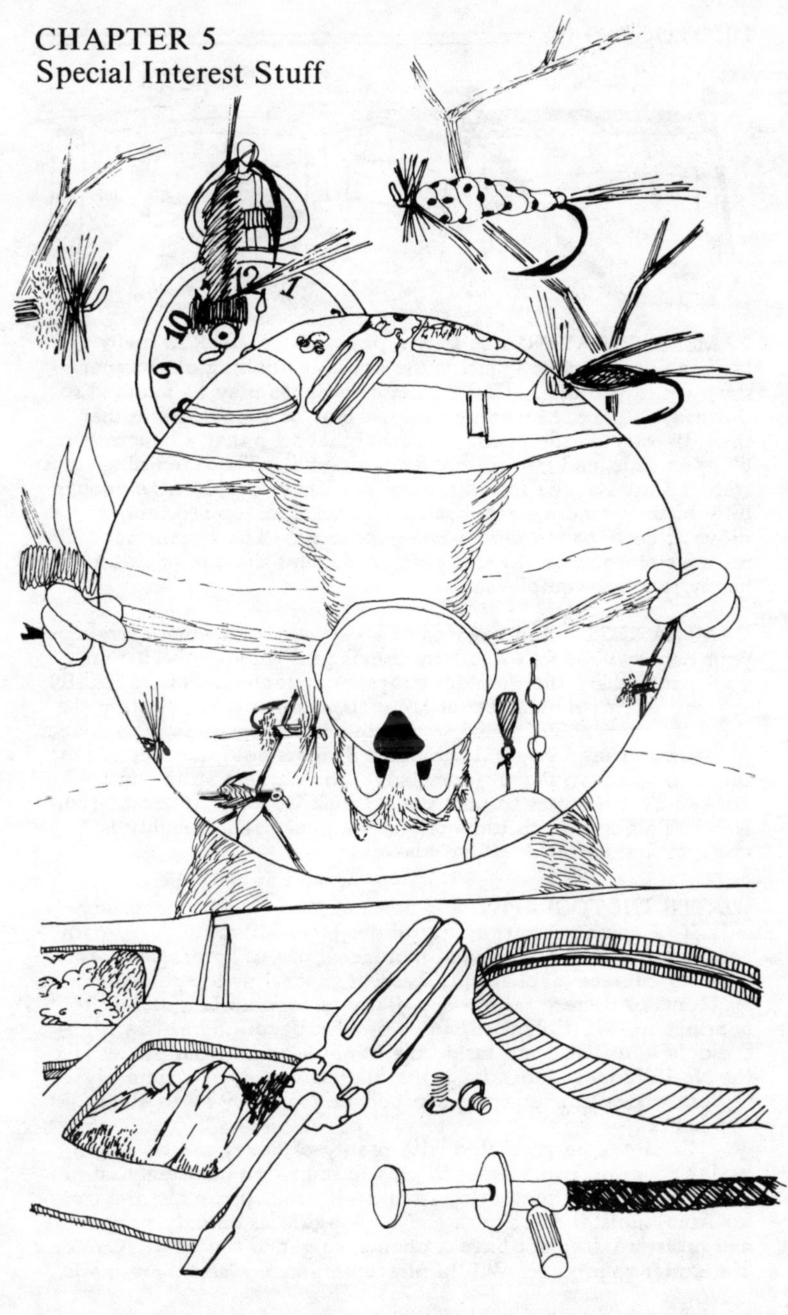

CAMERA CARRYING - A literal pain-in-the-neck to many backpacking photographers is the constant rubbing of a camera strap while walking. Certain kinds of packs may be adapted so the strap is placed around extension bars on the frame, rather than directly on the neck. For my JanSport pack, I bought two 6" extensions and cut off and discarded 5". The remaining stubs were inserted at the top of the pack. They are just high enough to hold the camera strap, and yet I can reach comfortably to move it down to my neck when necessary. The system not only relieves pressure on my neck but also keeps the camera within handy reach for quick use.

CAMERA PEGS - Another way to save your neck when carrying your camera: Insert extra long clevis pins through the bar on your pack where the shoulder straps are attached. There usually are one or two unused sets of holes there for use in adjusting the shoulder straps. Then find some kind of tubing to act as a spacer. (This reader used surgical tubing.) Spacers hold the tops of the clevis pins above the shoulder bar. The camera strap can be hooked over the pins to take the pressure off of your neck. (Ed. Note: This system should work on all packs and probably is cheaper and easier than that above.)

WINTER PHOTOGRAPHY - Winterizing a camera is necessary only if temperatures are likely to drop to -30° or colder. With new kinds of lubrications and increasing use of "greaseless bearings" in camera mechanism, even at super-low temperatures problems of battery failure are likely to crop up long before the bearings freeze. Likewise, tales of film becoming brittle from the cold and shattering inside the camera come from places like the North Slope. Moisture is the biggest enemy, particularly in regions where temperatures can bounce from 20° F. to 40° F. in two hours.

Film can be protected with plenty of heavy plastic bags. Kodak 35 mm. film comes in plastic snap-cap canisters that provide almost ideal protection from moisture. Just make the transfer from canister to camera and back again as quickly as possible and moisture does not have a chance to get to the film. Cameras are harder to protect. While most cameras nowadays are made

almost entirely of non-corroding alloys or plastics, a few strate-
gic ratchets, springs and screws still must be made of steel. Not
much moisture is needed to transform those parts into blobs of
rust, reducing the camera to an impressive but otherwise useless
conversation piece. Another problem is condensation of moisture
on the interior surfaces of the lenses. The thin film of water
droplets is inside so it cannot be wiped off. It prevents any picture from being taken and it can only be removed, short of completely disassembling the lens, by slowly baking the lens in an
oven at 100° F. for an evening.

While traveling, the camera can be wrapped in a double
layer of plastic bags and stashed in a protected part of the pack.
When the beautiful scenery is reached, though, the camera must
be brought out of its cocoon to face the elements. Simply keeping the case on at all times, only opening it for the short period
of time when the picture is actually being taken, provides quite
a bit of protection. Another method for keeping the camera dry
is to punch two holes in the bottom of a plastic bag and thread
the camera strap through the holes so that when traveling the bag
drops down over the camera. When a picture needs to be taken
the bag can be slid up the strap, uncovering the camera. The
bag tends to get in the way a bit, but it does keep the rain off
better than most cases and in addition protects the camera from
the moisture coming through the photographer's clothing. Using
both the bag and the case provides very good protection.

Using a tripod is good practice in any photography. It keeps
the camera steady and permits the photographer to give his full
attention to framing the picture and determining the proper exposure settings. On the trek in, the tripod can be strapped on the
pack frame. Arriving in picturesque territory, the tripod is un-
strapped and the camera mounted on it. If the rain is coming
down, a plastic bag quickly goes over the camera. With a little
practice, when a picture is found the tripod can be set up and the
major adjustments of height and camera angle made before pulling off the plastic bag.

Ideally, the procedure for taking a picture is to quickly
yank off the plastic bag, adjust the tripod, frame the picture,
focus the lens, take a light reading and make the exposure settings, push the shutter release and get the bag back in place --
all between one raindrop and the next. This ideal cannot always
be achieved. A few cotton handkerchiefs come in handy for
soaking up the raindrops that move faster than the photographer.

Condensation on lenses and viewfinders presents another
problem. Warm air holds more moisture than cold air. Since
when warm air comes in contact with a cold object the air will
be cooled, moisture will tend to condense on the cold object.
Thus, when you breathe on a cold lens moisture condenses on the
lens. Likewise, when a photographer tries to protect his cold
camera from the rain by putting it underneath his jacket, the
entire camera becomes covered with a thin film of moisture.

The best tactic for preventing condensation on optics is to
try to keep the camera at the same temperature as the outdoors.

When traveling, pack it on the outer part of the pack, away from body heat and moisture. When taking pictures, keep the camera outside of the clothing and away from openings in the clothing that will give off warm, moist air. Controlled breathing also is necessary when working with a cold camera. A sniff or a snort at the wrong time, when your head is close to the viewfinder, can create a film of water droplets on the optics that may take 10 minutes to evaporate.

If, despite all precautions, the camera really gets wet, such as if you wake up in the morning to find your Rollei 35 sitting in the bottom of a 3" puddle in one corner of your tent, call a competent repair person immediately. If the camera has little commercial value he may say "bake it and see if you can get away with it." But if it is an expensive machine, the only safe route is to disassemble the whole thing and dry it piece by piece.

Winter scenes require some special thinking in taking exposure readings. When snow occupies a good part of the picture, simply setting the camera like the meter tells you is likely to produce underexposed pictures. Light meters are programmed to think they are looking at grey scenes. Because most scenes have just about as many bright parts as dark and therefore average out to a middle grey, the meter assumes that all scenes average out to grey and bases its calculations of exposure settings on that assumption. When the meter is pointed at a scene that is mostly white, such as a skier traversing a snow slope, more of the light illuminating the scene is reflected to the meter than normal, and the meter thinks the scene is brighter than it actually is. The meter then scientifically informs the photographer that the camera should be set at a shutter speed that is actually too high or an aperture that is too small.

The trick to getting correct exposure from a snow scene is to take the light reading off a part of the scene that is nearer to a light value halfway between the brightest and darkest part of the scene. Simply point the meter at a parka sleeve or a clump of trees instead of at a snow slope. Another method sometimes recommended is to set the ASA lower on the meter than required for the film being used. This method is guaranteed to lead to confusion both because the photographer may forget to reset the ASA dial when more normal scenes are encountered and because the correction factor varies from scene to scene.

Whatever method of determining exposure is used, chances are the photographer will have to go through a period of trial and error before he comes up with a method that works for him. A notebook can speed up the transition from confusion to consistency. Write down not just the specific settings but why those settings were chosen (example: increase exposure one stop because of snow) and any tricks or new gadgets that are being tried. When the pictures come back from processing, carefully compare notes to the results.

-- Excerpts from an article, "Techniques for a
Frosty Photographer," by Rick Ells

*

READER RESPONDS - There is just one point with which I differ
-- that "winterizing" a camera is not necessary unless anticipat-
ing temperatures of -30° or lower. From personal experience, I
would heartily recommend the special lubrication and servicing
for cameras to be out for any period in temperatures as balmy as
-10°. My initial experience with a frozen camera was during my
first winter in Wyoming. The camera had not been winterized,
and the repair costs were nearly 2/3 the purchase price of the
camera.

For anyone planning a winter trek to the frigid Rockies,
such a servicing investment would indeed be wise. Temperatures drop as low as -60° here and I have spent many gorgeous
days cross-country skiing and snowshoeing with my cameras when
it has been a brisk -20°. Any machinery subject to the rigors of
this 7200-ft. altitude and six-month winter has to have extra
TLC to even begin to perform properly. And to have a camera
winterized year around here is not a luxury, since snow and freezing temperatures can be expected any month of the year in the
high country.

CAMERA WARMER - A hand warmer can be used to keep a
camera or some other piece of equipment from freezing. Place
both in a common breathable container, as a pocket or bag.
Some care may be required to make sure parts of the equipment
don't get too hot.

CAMERA STEADIER - A walking stick or ice axe is a handy
companion for photographers taking close-up photos, where
longer exposures may result in shakey images. Frequently,
there is nothing solid available at the desired vantage point.
A walking stick, however, often can be propped between a log
and a rock or whatever, to help brace the camera. Don't expect major miracles, but the extra assist might be the difference between a useable photo and the wastebasket.

CARRYING CASE - While camping or backpacking, a case for
your camera is almost a necessity to keep dirt and moisture out
of the mechanism and off the lens. One hiker struggled for many
years without a case since the commercial one available was
awkward and expensive. Finally he decided to use an old Blue-
Foam pad to try to solve the problem. The project took a few
hours of trial and error cutting, and a few yards of grey duct
tape, but the result was a lightweight (4 ozs.) enclosure which
protects the camera snugly from unavoidable bumps. A plastic
sack over the case keeps out rain and dirt. The next project
was to make a nylon covering with Velcro tabs to replace the
plastic sack.

The finished case "is a little bulky and provokes some odd stares and comments on the trail, but it is well worth the few hours and few dollars for the pad. (The remnant of the pad was large enough for a sitting pad.) The specialized case also would work if you are using a large, wide-angle or telephoto lens which doesn't fit the conventional leather case."

EASY CLOSE-UPS - It is possible to improvise and get close-up shots without the need for extension tubes and bellows attachments. Focus at infinity, then remove the lens from the camera body and reverse it, holding the front of the lens against the camera body with your hand, moving the camera back and forth until the image is in focus. (If you're lucky, you may be able to find a lens reverser ring which screws onto the front of the lens and, when the lens is reversed, attaches to the camera body.)

One photographer uses a Lentar reverser ring (bayonet-type mount) to hold a reversed Hanimex zoom lens to his Canon FTb body, and uses the zoom ring for focusing. Using a reversed zoom lens is also versatile because you are not limited to a single camera-to-subject distance; simply move the camera farther away or closer to the subject and refocus with the zoom ring.

If you are holding the lens against the camera body with your hand, make sure that your hand is steady and that stray light does not enter. Also, a wise precaution is to cover the lens with a UV or Skylight filter to prevent scratching it. Obviously the automatic aperture of the lens will not work using this technique, although built-in meter readings will still be accurate.

TECHNIQUE - Some general rules on technique which the backpacking photographer also will want to remember:

LEAN ON SOMETHING - A tree, a rock, a car, a tripod; anything to steady the camera. Propping yourself against something not only prevents vibrations that will ruin otherwise good pictures, but it gives you the time to give your full attention to properly framing and exposing the picture. Trying to catch a picture "on the fly" means trying to combine the processes of focusing, framing, exposing and steadying into one simultaneous act. Most people just can't do that many things at once.

EXPOSE CORRECTLY - In most cases, consistently getting the right exposure is simply a matter of avoiding "guestimating." Make it a point to take a light meter reading for every single photo. Also, pay close attention to what the meter is pointed at. Be sure you are taking the reading off of an important part of the picture and not letting some unusually bright or dark area confuse the meter.

KNOW YOUR EQUIPMENT - In addition to learning the function of each little dial, lever and button, each photographer must go through a period of familiarization with the particular camera. One must learn which way to turn the lens when focusing, so it can be done without thought. The amount of pressure needed to set off the shutter release should also come naturally, so the shutter opens at exactly the right instant. The muscles need to get used to the machine.

Accessories such as tripods, extension tubes and extra lenses can be just as complicated as the camera to use and will require just as much effort to test out and become familiar with.

KEEP ORGANIZED - Camera gear should be organized into some kind of a system. A kit containing everything likely to be needed is a good way to be sure that the right device is handy at the right time.

SEND FILM OFF IMMEDIATELY - Film should be processed as soon as possible after exposure. Not only does this prevent the emulsion from undergoing any changes from heat or humidity, but the photographer can see the results while he can still remember what he did.

Film should be sent to the same processor each time since different processors have slightly different methods which result in slight variations in the final pictures. Otherwise you might go bananas trying to figure out what you are doing wrong.

Instead of just dropping the film off, seek out the company that actually does the processing and see if it handles retail orders. The closer you get to them, the more likely you are to be dealing with people who know what they are talking about and have a stake in giving you good results.

*

DEVICES - Some devices which help make photography simpler and easier:

AUTOMATIC EXPOSURE CAMERAS - Automatic exposure systems in cameras are becoming more sophisticated. They usually are at least as reliable and accurate as the metering technique of most amateur photographers, providing a simple way to get over the hurdle of exposure settings, permitting more attention to the esthetics of the picture. For a person whose main interest is not in photography but still wants to get good, properly exposed photos now and then, the auto-cameras are great.

Examples of automatic cameras are the Olympus 35RC, the Yashica Electro, the Konica Autoreflex, the Nikkormat EL and the Pentax Spotmatic ES.

AUTOMATIC ELECTRONIC FLASH UNITS - Photography with conventional flash units has always been complicated by the problem of calculating the correct f-stop settings. With the new automatic flash units, instead of the photographer adjusting the f-stop to compensate for changes in the distance between light source and subject, the flash unit automatically controls the duration of the flash to make the correction. A small sensing cell on the front of the flash unit measures the amount of light being reflected back from the subject while the flash is actually occuring. If too much light is coming back, the circuitry cuts the flash short. To use these units, the camera is simply set at a specified f-stop, depending on the ASA of the film, and within a limited range of distances the flash unit will automatically give correct exposures.

CLOSE-UP LENSES - Close-up photography using extension tubes or bellows units requires calculating exposure compensation for extension, which someone who only wants to shoot an occasional flower or insect may not want to get into. Close-up lenses are simply magnifying lenses that screw onto the front of the camera lens. They do not require exposure compensation, but can be used to produce fairly high magnifications. They usually come in sets of three, each of a different magnification, and can be used singly or combined for higher magnifications.

THROUGH-THE-LENS METERS - Most single lens reflex cameras available today have built-in metering systems; the sensor cell is inside so it measures the light that will actually reach the film. For photographs taken with normal lenses at normal distances, putting the cell inside the camera does not make much difference, but when very long lenses are used or close-ups are being taken a through-the-lens metering system saves a lot of hassle. With close-ups, for example, high magnification is usually achieved by increasing the distance between the lens and film with extension tubes or a bellows unit. As that distance is increased, however, the exposure must be increased because the image becomes dimmer and dimmer. Without a TTL metering system the correction must be laboriously calculated. With a TTL meter, the photographer only has to center the needle and shoot. Anyone buying an SLR should be sure the camera has a TTL metering system.

-- Excerpts from the booklet, "Basic Photography, A Course Summary," by Rick Ells, Reprinted with Permission

FISHING TRICKS

KITCHEN UTENSIL SCALES FISH - I would like to pass along a little trick that has anything beat I have ever seen to scale fish. Just run some warm water over the fish and then use a Chore Boy scrubber (used for cleaning pots), and the scales come off like nothing. Beats a knife all hollow.

MOUNTAIN TROUT FISHING - Standard equipment for mountain lake fishing includes the following: 5- to 6-ft. ultralight or light action spinning rod, ultralight or lightweight spinning reel or spincasting reel, a spool of 2-lb. monofilament line, a spool of 4-lb. monofilament line, six 8-oz. spoons in assorted patterns (try two brass, two nickel and one each red-and-white and orange or pink), one 1-1/2" diameter snap-on bobber, six size 12 dryflies (one each Royal Coachman Fanwing, Cowdung, Black Gnat, White Miller, Spruce Fly and Spider), a dozen size 12 salmon egg

hooks, one tube of BB split shot, one tube No. 2 split shot, a
dozen snap swivels (size 10 or 12) and a jar of salmon eggs. With
this basic tackle, you can still fish, flyfish, cast lures, troll or
whatever.

GENERAL STRATEGY - Fish near drop-off areas such as
where rockslides enter the water. Shade and food in these areas
attract trout. Watch for surface feeding trout -- rings on the
water such as a thrown rock makes. Cast or walk to within casting distance of them. Cast parallel to the shoreline if using bob-
bers and bait or small lures such as spoons and spinners. Fish often will hide near rocks, logs and under overhanging brush. Work
inlet and outlet stream areas hard. Both are prime feeding areas
for trout.

Concentrate on early morning and late evening hours when
trout usually feed best in high lakes. If you fish during a sunny
mid-day period, bait would be the best choice as trout will be
hiding in the shady areas and reluctant to chase lures. If you do
spot trout feeding during mid-day, your chances of catching them
are good. Use light tackle and small diameter line -- 2- or 4-lb.
test monofilament is best. Line of greater diameter will reduce
your chances as high lake trout are finicky and spook easily.

TACTICS AND TACKLE -- In drop-off areas use either
baits or lures. Baits which produce best in high lakes are salmon
eggs and worms. Worms, admittedly, are tough to pack in as the
heat usually gets to them on a long hike. Salmon eggs are more
easily carried and heat won't bother them. I prefer cheese eggs
or light orange colored ones. If you are able to get worms into
the mountains, on a short hike for example, they will catch
plenty of fish and probably outdo salmon eggs.

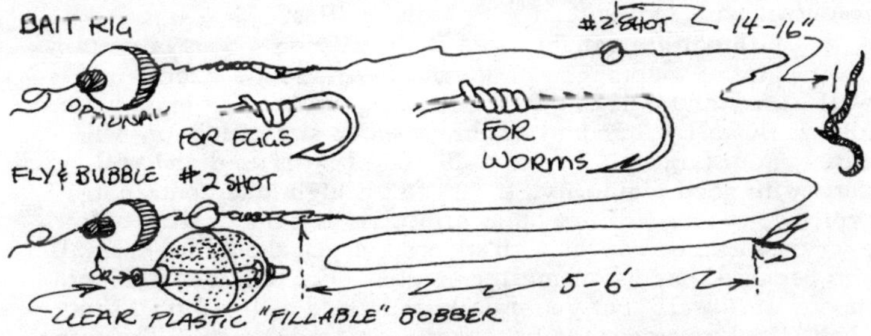

For bait fishing rig your line with a No. 2 split shot 14-16"
up from the hook and tie on a No. 12 egg hook or No. 8 worm
hook. Cast the rig as far as you can and let it settle to the bottom. Take in the slack line, prop the rod up on a rock or stick
and wait for a few minutes. If a trout doesn't take the bait, reel
in a few turns of line, let the rig again settle to the bottom and
sit for another five minutes. Repeat until bait can be seen; reel
in and cast out again. Small spoons and spinners are best fished
in drop-off areas by casting out, letting them sink for several
seconds, then slowly retrieving them. Experiment with different
depths before you move to another spot, and be sure to make
some parallel casts to the bank on either side of you.

In fishing for surface feeding trout the fly and bubble technique is best. These fish are after a particular insect on the surface and flies will fool them better than spoons or baits. Size 12 dry flies in dark colors work best. Attach a 1-1/2" bobber 4-6' up the line and tie on a dry fly at the end. Use no weight between the fly and bobber. If extra weight is needed to increase casting distance, add split shot directly under the bobber where it will not affect the action of the fly on the end of the line. Cast the fly-and-bubble rig to the rings made by feeding trout and allow it to rest quietly on the water for several seconds. If a trout doesn't take the fly within a half-minute, reel in a few feet and let the fly rest again. Repeat this process until the fly is away from the rings, reel in and cast out again.

Inlet and outlet stream areas in a high lake generally are shallow, but food conditions are optimum. You will probably find all methods effective -- fly and bubble, bait on the bottom, and casting small lures. Regardless of the fishing method used in these areas, remember that trout spook easily and the shallow water enables them to see you better than if they were in deeper water. Pick a spot near brush or a tree or large rock from which to cast.

TROUT TRICKS - Of the three basic fishing methods, spoon fishing probably is the easiest to learn. Once you've mastered the art of casting with your spinning outfit, you've practically learned how to fish with spoons as they are continually cast out and retrieved. But there are tricks to catching high lake trout with spoons. Cutthroat and brook trout lakes are prime territory as these species will hit spoons more readily than rainbow. Although caught consistently with spoons, rainbow are much harder to outwit with spoons than with baits or flies.

Cutthroat are caught more frequently on spoons of certain color patterns -- orange, pink and chartreuse are excellent, as well as red-and-white. On sunny days, nickel and brass patterns also work well. Standard cutthroat spoon size of 1/8-oz. will cast long distances if 2- and 4-lb. test line is used and will catch cutts with good regularity. If you fish a high lake containing rainbow, spoons will not be as effective as baits or flies. However they can be caught with spoons but you should use a smaller size because they have smaller mouths. For rainbow, 1/16-oz. spoons work well, but you usually must add a No. 2 split shot above the lure to get the necessary casting distance. The same color patterns used for cutthroat will work. The split shot will spook the fish unless it is far enough ahead of the lure so they can't see it; 2-3' is generally far enough. Brook trout will hit spoons readily. The 1/8-oz. size is recommended and the red-and-white color pattern is by far the best.

Spoon fishing technique is to cast the lure to a likely area (drop-offs, near inlet and outlet streams, near rockslides and close to shore near snags, shady areas and brush), let it sink several seconds and then begin a slow and steady retrieve. If no strikes occur there are several things you can try. First, change the retrieve speed, alternating between fast and slow every five seconds. If fish still ignore the spoon, try retrieving slow and

steady but with short, sharp jerks every few feet. You probably
will wish to attach a snap swivel to the spoon to prevent line
twist and allow fast changes of spoon size and color patterns.
Unfortunately, snap swivels often spook mountain lake trout. If
you are having difficulty catching fish, remove the snap swivel
and tie the line directly to the lure. Remember, you will now
have to allow the lure to hang in the air several feet below the
rod tip to untwist the line before making each cast.

A final note about spoon fishing. Always assume that high
lake trout can be at any depth. Near a rockslide area, try one
cast and start retrieving immediately to keep the spoon near the
surface. On each successive cast, allow it to sink two seconds
longer, until on one cast the line will hit the bottom and go
slack. Repeat this different depth casting process twice for each
area of water fished until you find the correct depth, and then
stick with it. Surface feeding cutthroat and brook trout will hit
spoons readily if the lure is cast beyond them and retrieved close
to the surface through the feeding area, but rainbow generally
won't pay much attention to this method.

FLY FISHING - Mountain trout rely heavily on insects for
food and the hair and feather fly is nothing more than an imitation of this natural food. The problem is how to fish them. I
do quite a bit of stream fly fishing myself, but have found fly
fishing outfits quite unmanageable when it comes to high lakes.
The biggest problem is finding enough room to backcast, and in
most lakes I've been to you wind up fighting more tree limbs and
brush than fish. The solution: adapt your spinning outfit by using the fly and bubble technique.

With an ultralight spinning outfit and 2- or 4-lb. test monofilament line, you can easily cast a fly and bubble outfit to
feeding trout. No problem finding a lot of room to backcast,
and you have the option of fishing baits or spoons with the same
outfit. Tie one of the flies suggested earlier to the end of your
line and then attach a 1-1/2" snap-on bobber (the red-and-white
will do just fine) 5' up the line from the fly. In casting, you
will find the almost weightless fly will not foul up despite the
long length of line between it and the bobber. If you have trouble casting far enough, crimp a No. 2 split shot directly beneath
the bobber for additional weight.

Cast to spots where fish are feeding, allow the fly to rest
on the surface for a second or two and then begin a slow but
steady retrieve. If trout won't strike the fly in this manner, on
the next cast move the fly a few feet, stop reeling, move it another few feet, stop and so on. If trout still are finicky, try retrieving in short jerks. Next switch fly patterns until you find
one they like. Besides the obvious spots to fish -- where trout
are rising to feed on surface insects -- try near outlet and inlet
stream areas, parallel casts to the shoreline and near logs and
other good hiding areas.

Flies also may be fished effectively from rubber or log
rafts. The same fly patterns are also good for trolling, plus
size 12 Royal Coachman Bucktails, Carey Specials and Brown

Hackles. Flyrods can be used but, again, the multi-purpose
ultralight spinning outfit will do a fine job and save the additional pack-in weight. My personal preference in trolling flies
is to use no weight at all, but if fish aren't actively feeding on
the surface the addition of a No. 2 split shot several feet ahead
of the fly should produce strikes. Aside from that, rubber rafts
do spook trout so it's important to troll far enough behind the
boat so trout can't see you -- 50' should be adequate but if
strikes aren't coming try letting out more line. For raft fly
trolling, the important thing is to keep the boat moving. A
slow, steady rowing speed with starts and stops mixed in will
outwit most trout.
-- Excerpts from "Mountain Trout Tactics," Signpost
Bulletin No. 13, by John Thomas

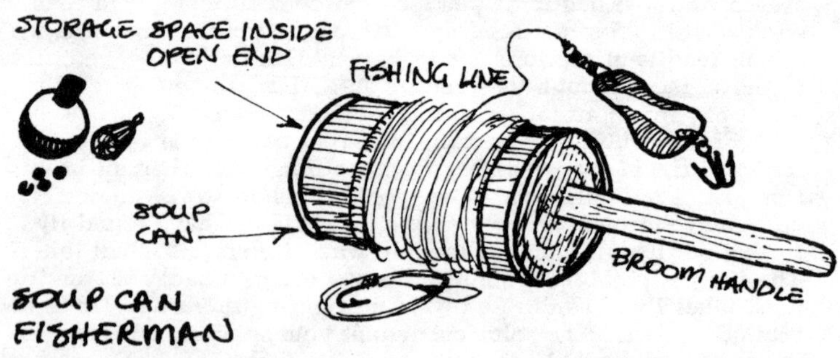

SOUP CAN FISHERMAN

CANNED FISHERMAN - A wandering college professor told of
Indians in Chile who use tin cans to catch fish. We tried it, developed the idea a little and came up with the Canned Fisherman. All you need is a can (regular Campbell soup can is a
good size), a plastic snap lid to fit the top of the can, a wood
screw and washer, six inches of 1" wood doweling, some electri-
cian's tape, a plastic Kodak snap-cap film can (available at any
camera store), and your hook, line and sinker.

Using the wood screw and washer, attach one end of the
dowel to the bottom of the can. Tie one end of the fish line
around the can and anchor it firmly with tape; then wrap the rest
of the line around the can. When traveling, the bobber, hook
and sinker end of the line are kept inside the can, held there by
the plastic lid. Extra hooks, etc., kept in the film can, also
can be carried along inside the soup can container.

To cast with the Canned Fisherman, you go through about
the same long-arm, overhand motion you would to throw a Ger-
man potato masher type grenade, except you don't let go. The
line reels off the can exactly as it would from a good spinning
reel.

The Canned Fisherman is as durable as the components used
in its construction, and it is the kind of device that can be repaired by simply bending it back to approximately the right
shape. Its casting and reeling accuracy are not quite up to the
pocket-type fishing equipment you buy, but it has about the

same casting range. Creating a Canned Fisherman costs about
$2. Only about 8" long, it's easy to pack. A cheap and easy
way to take advantage of fishing opportunities along the trail and
get a line out to the right spot.

ROD REPAIRS - Not much casting and reeling is needed to wear
down even the hardest guides on a fishing rod. Since the rod itself is usually affected little by such use, many fishermen find it
worth the effort to simply replace the guides rather than buying a
whole new pole. The Gudebrod Brothers Silk Company has a
small pamphlet that clearly explains the art of removing old
guides and replacing them with new ones. The folder gives a
detailed description of how to wrap the thread, how to tie it, and
how to finish it. You can request one by writing c/o Fishing
Tackle Division, 12 South 12th Street, Philadelphia, PA 19107.

WARM FEET - Here's a special tip to ice fishermen. Keep feet
warmer by spraying the bare feet with a strong anti-perspirant
before leaving home. This helps prevent sweating, and dry feet
don't get nearly as cold. This might even open a new field for
no-sweat products!

INDEX